PEACE CORPS CHRONOLOGY

1961–2010

SECOND EDITION

Lawrence F. Lihosit

iUniverse, Inc.
New York Bloomington

Peace Corps Chronology; 1961-2010
SECOND EDITION

iUniverse books may be ordered through booksellers or by contacting:

iUniverse
1663 Liberty Drive
Bloomington, IN 47403
www.iuniverse.com
1-800-Authors (1-800-288-4677)

ISBN: 978-1-4620-1700-3 (sc)
ISBN: 978-1-4620-1701-0 (dj)
ISBN: 978-1-4620-1702-7 (e)

Printed in the United States of America

iUniverse rev. date: 5/9/2011

Special thanks to–

Editor in Chief- Will James
Assistant Editor- Starley Talbott
Contributors- Marian Haley Beil, John Coyne, Chris Austin (staff for Rep. John Garamendi, D-CA), Stanley Meisler, Hugh Pickens, Joanne Roll, P. David Searles
Cover Photo- Dra. L. Margarita Solis Kitsu de Lihosit

In classical literature, heroes and heroines either die or are totally incapacitated as a consequence of their quest. This book is dedicated to the memory of those Peace Corps volunteers who died during or immediately following service to our nation and the world.

CONTENTS

Foreword by P. David Searles, Ph.D. ix

Preface. 1

Peace Corps Chronology. 7

Sources 61

Peace Corps Goals 71

Maps, Lists & Graphs 75
    Map 1: Mexico, C. & S. America 77
    Map 2: Caribbean Islands 78
    Map 3: Europe. 79
    Map 4: Africa 80
    Map 5: Middle East. 81
    Map 6: Asia. 82
    Map 7: Pacific Islands. 83
    List: Nations Served, Dates & Number of Volunteers 84
    Figure 1: % of volunteers by region 90
    List: Number of volunteers per year 91
    Figure 2: Average # of volunteers/decade 92
    Figure 3: Number of volunteers/year 92
    Figure 4: Average volunteer age/selected years 93
    Figure 5: % of volunteers per work sector/selected years . . . 94

About the Author 95

Index 99

FOREWORD

A lot can happen in fifty years, as demonstrated by this superb book. Lihosit has carefully sifted through an immense cache of Peace Corps data from a wide variety of sources, some of which are familiar and some of which were previously unknown to me. In the book, he gives a detailed account of the critical happenings– year by year, decade by decade, from 1961 to the present.

The book will be read in two ways. The first, and this is probably what most of us former volunteers and staff will immediately do, is to check out what he has included from our years with the Peace Corps. For me that meant 1971 through 1976 and I say he got the important points very well. The second way –and this is of more importance– is to use the material in the book to track both the significant changes that have occurred over fifty years and the matters that have remained untouched throughout the same period. Some of the changes he records are remarkable. The ratio of men to women volunteers is now the reverse of what it was in the beginning. Volunteer isolation in remote work sites –the norm early on– has been alleviated dramatically by the advent of new communications technologies. An unheard of health problem in my time (HIV/AIDS) has become both a significant personal concern and a valuable and much appreciated area of Volunteer work. Happily, Lihosit's data indicates that at long lost the very worrisome problem of early terminations has lessened. Readers will find evidence of any number of similarly important changes –as one would expect over fifty years– and then be able to puzzle whether or not the changes are good or bad.

On the other hand, it is a bit disturbing to learn that some of the major problems encountered in the early years remain. The Peace Corps still struggles with the question of how best to recruit, train and support Volunteers. The federal government has more often than not failed to provide adequate budgets for the Peace Corps. Too often staff appointments reflect political connections rather than a person's personal commitment to "making the world a better place." The merits of the five-year rule continue to be hotly debated, and often ignored, despite an open and shut case for it, in my opinion. Perhaps the most disturbing fact that Lihosit has produced is that the Washington-based bureaucracy now sucks up a much greater portion of the agency's resources than it has done historically. The growth in Washington staff alone is enough to make a fellow think seriously about becoming a Tea-Partier!

In the preface, Lihosit makes a strong case for the establishment of a permanent home for Peace Corps material such as books (including self-published ones), personal memoirs, official documents, photos, art– everything and anything that has a Peace Corps connection. He favors housing the collection in the Library of Congress which seems right to me. Elsewhere he makes another strong case for doing something to combat the rising tide of violence directed at Volunteers, especially women. Finally, he has dedicated this book to the Volunteers who have given their lives in Peace Corps service. This is a fine gesture and in fact is a belated recognition of an occurrence which has been far more common than most of us realize.

P. David Searles. Ph.D.
Country Director (71-74) & Deputy Director (74-76)
December 13, 2010

PREFACE

Good ideas, like a stick of gum, need to be chewed on for a while. American unarmed service abroad is no exception. During the first term of former Rough Rider Theodore Roosevelt, American philosopher William James first seeded the idea in Boston. Sharing the stage with Jane Addams of Chicago's Hull House for an address to the Universal Peace Conference, James counseled that "We must go in for preventive medicine, not radical cure." He repeated similar themes in subsequent speeches in 1906 and 1910. He believed that mankind would only find peace through self-sacrifice and example.

Forty-eight years later, following two world wars, Senator Brien McMahon (D-Connecticut) spoke about "missionaries of democracy." Five more years passed before Senator Hubert Humphrey (D-Minnesota) introduced a bill to create a Peace Corps. According to the Senator, "It did not meet much enthusiasm." Maybe, but folks kept chewing and thinking. In July, 1958 Congressman Henry S. Reuss (D-Wisconsin) and Senator Richard L. Neuberger (D-Oregon) introduced measures calling for a study about the "Point Four Youth Corps." This referred to former President Harry Truman's Point Four Program which offered technical assistance to underdeveloped nations in Africa, Asia and Latin America. Reuss and Neuberger hoped that a volunteer corps element working abroad might improve

America's image. Their idea was incorporated into the Mutual Security Appropriation Act as an amendment in August, 1960, only weeks after John F. Kennedy had been nominated by the Democratic Party as its candidate for the Presidency. That summer, a research group in Colorado was selected to prepare a study.

During the Presidential campaign, Kennedy made a late night campaign stop at the University of Michigan where he asked a group of college students if they would serve overseas. The response from the group as well as around the nation was positive. Kennedy requested that Max Millikan and Chester Bowles outline an organization and goals. Within two weeks he adopted this into his campaign, speaking in favor of a Peace Corps. His staff began contacting the Colorado study group almost immediately, asking whether the study would be completed by February.

Per the Mutual Security Appropriations Act, the Colorado State University Research Foundation in Fort Collins was contracted to prepare the study. Signed only one week after Kennedy's election, the report was to include the study of "at least 10 countries, on three continents" in terms of suitability for an overseas volunteer program.

Five days before the Presidential inauguration, Maurice Albertson, Andrew E. Rice and Pauline E. Birky of the Colorado State University Research Foundation were briefed in Washington D.C. by the State Department then left on separate assignments to begin negotiations for an overseas Peace Corps. Albertson flew to Pakistan, Rice to Africa and Birky to Mexico, Colombia, Haiti and Chile. On January 20, 1961, President John F. Kennedy addressed the nation and made this simple request: "Ask not what your country can do for you—ask what you can do for your country."

Less than 50 days later, the Peace Corps began. This tome includes a brief summary of notable activities related to what has become an iconic part of our foreign policy. Nearly fifty years after its inception, many of the boundaries and even names of countries where volunteers served have changed. The world is much more urban and communications are instantaneous. The Corps has changed as well. Volunteers are now older, more experienced and mostly female. There are more volunteers over the age of 50 and more volunteers from each part of our American patch-work quilt. The agency itself has experimented with a wide array of changes to selection, training, jobs and even organization. For example, Peace Corps strategies and work plans include cooperation with other agencies like USAID as well as international non-governmental organizations. Many of those changes are noted in this chronology as are pertinent facts about volunteers and the places where they have served in. Some of the changes proved transitory. For instance, selection originally targeted young college graduates with outstanding academic careers and volunteer leadership positions. Within ten years, as the agency sought older, more experienced technicians, academic superiority was not emphasized. Most recently, the average volunteer has had a 3.6 college Grade Point Average and 94% have held some sort of school leadership position. Other changes, like an older volunteer, have been true for a generation. Likewise, the attrition rate of volunteers who leave before completing their term is about the same as it was in the early 1960's. One of the unfortunate changes has been to cut training. which consisted of 16 weeks in 1967 and again in 1979 to 10 to 12 weeks. Cutting language training hampers the volunteer for learning a foreign language is the most important element.

Since the first goal of the Peace Corps is to provide technical assistance for those nations that request it, the volunteer jobs have evolved as the needs have changed. There is much more emphasis on business today compared to the beginning. However, the relative number of teachers and health workers is very similar. Young Americans still teach English and help fight disease.

All contributors were surprised by the number of volunteer so have died while in service. This is a fact not widely publicized. Analysis of volunteer death rates is extremely difficult but two trends are apparent. The greatest number of deaths during the past 49 years are attributed to accidents and of these motor vehicle accidents are the most common cause of death. While this rate has decreased, there has been an alarming increase of assaults and even murder of volunteers dating back to 1992. Many of the assaults were sexual in nature and targeted young female volunteers who now represent the majority. To date, the Peace Corps has not taken prevention seriously. Volunteers should be given an hour a day of self-defense class during training and supplied with shrill whistles and small canisters of pepper spray which any camper in the United States would carry. Since most victims of sexual assault. are young females serving alone in tiny villages, it might be wise to assign them in pairs-the buddy system.

Measuring success has always been controversial. The three main goals (to offer technical assistance to nations who request it, to help foreigners understand Americans and to help Americans to understand foreigners) are difficult to quantify. However, the number of nations where the Peace Corps left and was later invited back is surprising. Likewise the number of volunteers who trudge home to write a book about their experience is equally surprising, one in two hundred. Many Americans speak proudly about our constitutional right to a free press yet very few practice the art of writing and publication. Ninety percent of these Peace Corps experience memoirs are published at the author's expense. There are now hundreds of memoirs in print and thousands of other types of books written by volunteers. When reading former volunteer's memoirs, one notes similarities: loneliness, difficulty understanding and adapting to a foreign culture and language, the constant battle to maintain good health and gratefulness for the opportunity to experience something different in exchange for work (much like the CCC for another generation). While this book offers a thumb-nail sketch, the real portraits are available in Peace Corps memoirs.

Almost since its inception, different institutions have discussed a permanent Peace Corps Library and Museum. Ironically, the majority of research for this chronology was not based upon any institution but rather privately funded electronic sites, obscure books purchased at Peace Corps reunions (which are rarely accepted into university library collections since they are not commercially published), interviews, and newspaper and magazine articles copied at local libraries. The Peace Corps once had its own library. As late as 1989 it had a library with books, magazines, pamphlets and even a librarian. Sometime before 1995 it was unceremoniously dismantled. Nobody seems really sure what actually happened to the collection-there are several versions. As we approach the fiftieth anniversary of the Peace Corps' inception, government documents are most probably stored away somewhere in boxes, or on magnetic tape, or Microfiche, or

4

even on transparent rolls of microfilm, quietly disintegrating. The memoirs so carefully written and published by our own citizens are scattered over the nation like blowing leaves, to be lost. On the official Peace Corps web site, this message was recently posted; "Our resources do not permit us to serve as a comprehensive Peace Corps historic archive, nor is it our mandate to do so." Unfortunately, it is nobody's mandate. I suggest that Congress mandate the Library of Congress to immediately begin a Peace Corps Experience Special Collection based upon donations of published volunteer and staff letters, journals, memoirs, essays, novels, short stories, plays, poetry and/or songs. In this way we can ensure that future generations can share this wonderful experiment in unarmed foreign policy. It would also fulfill the Peace Corps third goal to help Americans understand foreigners.

Since 2008, Fort Collins, Colorado (former home of the Colorado State University Research Foundation) has been soliciting funds for a different type of fulfillment. They intend to build a Peace Corps Museum to house art from around the planet. A small theater and two classrooms will be open to the public for meetings, receptions and educational field trips.

Lawrence F. Lihosit
June 21, 2010

PEACE CORPS CHRONOLOGY

1960's: The Beginning

(Note: all countries referred to with 2010 names. Former names are included within the list of countries served.)

1961

Mar. 1, 1961   President John F. Kennedy signed an Executive Order creating the Peace Corps. He hoped to have 500 volunteers in the field by year's end.

Mar. 4, 1961   Robert Sargent Shriver Jr, Kennedy's brother-in-law, was appointed the first Peace Corps Director. "I think the Peace Corps is beginning to remove doubts...I have been impressed." Sen. Barry Goldwater (R-AZ)

May 15, 1961   Colorado State University Research Foundation presented their final report. The first placement test was administered.

Jun., 1961   *Peace Corps News* first published.

Aug. 28, 1961 The first countries to request technical assistance were: Ghana, Nigeria, and Tanzania, India, Pakistan, Malaysia, Thailand, Colombia, Chile, St. Lucia, and the Philippines.

In an effort to weed out potential problems the Peace Corps instituted an entrance exam to fit psychological profiles. Training was done within the United States and included "team-building" physical activities similar to those used by airborne rangers. Trainees were monitored by psychologists. Training included approximately 50 hours of language class as well as "instruction in the philosophy, strategy, tactics, and the menace of communism." (Section 8(c), Peace Corps Act)

The first groups of Peace Corps Volunteers sent to Ghana and Tanzania, Africa.

Sept. 22, 1961 Kennedy signed the Peace Corps Act.

Oct. 13, 1961 A postcard written by a Peace Corps Volunteer in Nigeria was intercepted in that country and publicized. Within it, the volunteer described that country as squalid and primitive. Nigerian college students protested, calling Peace Corps Volunteers "spies," the program a tool of neo-colonialism and demanded deportation. False accusations that volunteers were spies would be repeated for the next half century. The volunteer was returned to the U.S.A. The program continued. However, volunteers were now taught to guard their own opinions. This incident would be described to all Peace Corps Trainees for many years.

Fall, 1961   Of the 12,644 applications, 913 participated in training. Nearly one in five (18%) did not finish training. An additional one in ten (10%) would not complete two years of service. This is the lowest worldwide attrition rate ever recorded (26%). Three-quarters of those who reported for training completed two years of service. The average volunteer age was 24.5 years.

8

Dec., 1961   These programs opened: Chile, Colombia, St. Lucia, Ghana, Tanzania, Nigeria, Pakistan and the Philippines.

1962

Jan., 1962   *The Volunteer* was first published. This had a newspaper format and usually included 24 pages of articles with bylines.

Jun. 30, 1962 Worldwide, volunteers totaled 2,940.

Dec., 1962   These programs opened: Tunisia, Turkey, Belize, Bolivia, Brazil, Dominican Republic, Ecuador, El Salvador, Jamaica, Peru, Venezuela, Cameroon, Ethiopia, Cote d'Ivoire, Liberia, Niger, Sierra Leone, Togo, Afghanistan, Cyprus, India, Iran, Malaysia, Nepal, Somali Republic, Sri Lanka, and Thailand.

These volunteers died during or immediately following service overseas: David Crozier & Lawrence Radley (Colombia), David Mulholland (Philippines), and Dale Swenson (Brazil).

1963

Spring, 1963 A special edition of *Peace Corps News* was used as a supplement used on college campuses for recruiting. Editors were all experienced journalists (including Roger Ebert) and the magazine was printed in a newspaper format.

Jun. 30, 1963 Volunteers totaled 6,646 serving in 45 countries. Early programs emphasized education, agriculture, health and community development. Worldwide, more than half were teachers (54.6%), a quarter worked in community development (25.6%), nearly one in ten worked in health (8.2%), with the same relative number working in agriculture (7.6%) and one in twenty worked in other (4.0%).

Peace Corps volunteer training still included 48 hours about communism. Charlie Peters, hired in 1962 as the Director of Evaluation remembered, "They were training volunteers to be junior diplomats…and expected them to argue with the communists. Well, they didn't run into many communists out there, just lots of poor peasants…The first thing we did was increase the language training from 50 to 250 hours and emphasize training in the host culture."

Dec., 1963   These programs opened: Costa Rica, Grenada, Guatemala, Honduras, Panama, Uruguay, Gabon, Guinea, Malawi, Senegal, Indonesia, and Morocco. No programs closed.

Four Peace Corps Volunteers were taken hostage for ten days by striking Bolivian miners.

These volunteers died during or immediately following service overseas: Nancy Boyd, Phillip Maggard and Roger McManua (Philippines) and Frederick Detjen (Colombia).

1964

Spring, 1964   Volunteers included 65% men and 35% women.

Jun. 30, 1964   Worldwide, volunteers totaled 10,078.

Fall, 1964   Peace Corps served 46 countries. The largest contingent served in Latin America where community development was the emphasis while the next largest contingent served in the Africa, followed by the Far East where education was the emphasis. Nearly half of all volunteers worked in Latin America (42%) followed by Africa (31%), Middle East/North Africa/South Asia (16%) and the Far East (11%).

Domestic peace corps, called Volunteers in Service to America (VISTA), was formed.

10

Dec. 1964   These programs opened: Uganda and Kenya. These programs closed: Sri Lanka and Cyprus.

These volunteers died during or immediately following service overseas: Bruce McKeen (Nepal) and Cynthia Myers (India).

1965

Mar.5-7, 1965 First National Returned Peace Corps Volunteers Conference was held in Washington, D.C.

Mar. 31, 1965 Of the volunteers worldwide, half were teachers (51.8%), one quarter were involved with community development (26.2%), one in ten were involved with health (9.9%) and nearly one in ten were involved with agriculture (7.9%). The remainder was involved with "other" work (4.2%).

Spring, 1965   In India, the development of a local poultry industry was emphasized. Eventually 1,200 volunteers served there at one time.

Jun. 30, 1965 Worldwide, volunteers totaled 13,248.

Aug., 1965   The leading causes of volunteer death were motorcycle and automobile accidents. The use of motorcycles was briefly banned.

Fall, 1965   The press noted culture shock among returning volunteers. Dr. Joseph English of the agency's medical division remarked that the condition was "overemphasized." However, changes were made. Prior to reporting to training, potential volunteers were sent to a live-in session (often on a college campus) lasting up to one week where they might be observed by professionals. Later called "staging," the effort was meant to lower attrition rates by sending home candidates believed to be bound for failure.

Dec., 1965   This program opened: Barbados. This program closed: Indonesia Prior to a military coup in Indonesia, the Indonesia program closed.

These volunteers died during or immediately following service overseas: Gareth Simmons & Robert Zech (Dominican Republic), Joy Darling (Bolivia), Don Humphrey (Chile), Stanley Kowalczyk & Johnnes Vonfoerster (Nigeria), Francis Kirking (Iran), James Hughes (Ecuador), John Parrott (Kenya), James Driscoll (Togo) and Judith Corley (Cameroon).

1966

Mar 1, 1966   Jack Vaughn succeeded Robert Sargent Shriver Jr as Director. He promoted conservation, natural resource management and community development. He improved Peace Corps marketing, programming and volunteer support.

Jun. 30, 1966   The number of Volunteers worldwide reached 15,556, the highest number ever, serving in 47 countries. To achieve this, 27% of applicants were invited to training. Attrition rates had risen each year as the number of volunteers. increased. By 1966, nearly half (47%) of all invited to train did not complete at least two years of service. Psychological testing during training was reduced and military style physical training dropped.

Male volunteers in the Philippines complained that volunteers there were being recalled during service and upon arrival in the U.S.A., pressed into military service.

Dec., 1966   These programs opened: Botswana, Chad, Libya, Marshall Islands, Micronesia, and South Korea. This program closed: Guinea.

These volunteers died during or immediately following service overseas: Curtis Larson, Paul Bond & Gerald Flynn (Ecuador),

Peverly Kinsey (Tanzania), William Olson (Ethiopia), Florice Barnum (Togo), Troy Ross (Peru), Thomas Hassett & Robert Weland (Nepal), James Redmann (E. Caribbean), Thomas Ashton (Iran), Lowell Dunn (Thailand), Henry George Shine and Diane Nitahara (Nigeria).

1967

Feb., 1967 The total number of volunteers older than 50. years equaled 340 or 1.6% of all volunteers who had served to date. Average volunteer age was 23.5 years.

Jun. 30, 1967 Worldwide, volunteers totaled 14,216.

Summer, 1967 Volunteers in Chile circulated a petition to protest the Vietnam War.. Jack Vaughn, Director, sent a letter to all countries assuring volunteers that they had the right to free speech but as public employees should avoid identification of those beliefs with their employer. "The Peace Corps...has neither the expertise nor the mission to address itself to political matters. It has no position..." he wrote. One of the volunteers wrote to the New York Times. When it did not print his letter, he had a Spanish version of the same letter printed in a Chilean newspaper. He was fired. He later filed suit in federal district court which ruled in his favor, limiting the Peace Corps' ability to punish volunteers for voicing opinions.

Jun., 1967 During the Middle East War Mauritania broke diplomatic relations with the U.S.A. The Mauritania program closed. Peace Corps announced it would close the Pakistan program as well.

Jun. 30, 1967 As the War in Vietnam escalated, Peace Corps appropriations shrank and with it, the number of volunteers began to decrease. Worldwide, volunteers totaled 14,968.

Jul., 1967 Civil War began in Nigeria and volunteers were evacuated from the war zone. A pilot training program was tested in Turkey rather than in the U.S.A. with the idea that trainees would learn more language in their host country.

In order to improve recruiting, Stanford graduates (former volunteers) became campus recruiters and the University of California Berkeley held its first informational meeting with possible recruits. Previously, Washington D.C. staff visited colleges and universities.

Nov., 1967   Volunteers in Honduras complained that of the 90 males serving as volunteers, two had received a Final Induction Notice and two others a Preliminary Induction Notice within one month. All four expected to be recalled to the U.S.A. and immediately pressed into military service.

Fall, 1967   In an address to all volunteers in Turkey, the Country Director stated that "disenchantment (among volunteers) sets in early...the Peace Corps intrudes too much." He went on to defend new rules. "Too many volunteers abdicated their individual responsibilities and rules became necessary." In particular, he cited volunteers who abused vacation policies.

Training periods were extended from between 12 and 14 weeks to 16 and 17 weeks

Dec., 1967   Placement (entrance) test dropped. The Peace Corps Library was created to serve staff, volunteers and the public.

These programs opened: Tonga, Western Samoa, Kiribati, Anguilla, Antigua/Barbuda, Dominica, Guyana, Montserrat, Paraguay, St. Christopher/Nevis, St. Vincent/the Grenadines, Burkina Faso, The Gambia, Lesotho, Mauritania and Sri Lanka. These programs closed: Gabon, Pakistan and Mauritania.

These volunteers died during or immediately following service overseas: David Larson (Dominican Republic), Dennis Pearson & Marcia Pearson (Turkey), Roseanne Crimmins & John Blum (India), William Reiser (Ghana), Bruce Gould (Philippines), James Stout, Jr (Morocco), Peter Nelson (Iran) and Susan Traub (Ethiopia).

1968

Mar. 1, 1968 "If you would confirm your faith in the American future–take a look at the Peace Corps," President Lyndon Baines Johnson in a letter to Congress.

Mar, 1968 Liechtenstein and Tonga issued stamps to commemorate U.S. Peace Corps programs in their countries. The Peace Corps served in 57 countries.

Jun. 30, 1968 Worldwide, volunteers totaled 13,823.

Oct., 1968 Mrs. Indira Gandhi, Prime Minister of India, accompanied 97 Peace Corps trainees on a flight to New Delhi from the U.S.A. During the flight she told them, "Having people come from outside is a help…It's going to create understanding."

Dec. 1968 An independent analysis of Peace Corps data prognosticated that nearly two-thirds (65%) of all volunteers who reported for training did not complete two years (attrition).

Almost half of all new volunteers had at least part of their training in-country.

These programs opened: Nicaragua, Benin and Fiji. No programs closed.

These volunteers died during or immediately following service overseas: William Hellyer (India), Mark Raymaker (Tanzania), Alexei Zbitnoff (El Salvador), Salvador Vazquez & William Ackerman (Colombia), John O'Brien (Fiji), John Beckner (Malaysia), Thomas Laffey (Malawi) and Virginia Zink (Nigeria).

1969

Winter, 1969 The United Nations General Assembly unanimously decided to study the creation of its own Peace Corps.

May 1, 1969   Joseph Blatchford succeeded Jack Vaughn as Peace Corps Director. He emphasized recruiting skilled volunteers (rather than "generalists" with little or no work experience) and instituted the Office of Returned Peace Corps Volunteers. He called his approach "New Directions." The plan included five objectives: recruiting older, skilled volunteers, dropping the ban on families, integration of service by placing volunteers more directly under the auspices of their host countries and hiring more foreign nationals in the overseas office.

The number of volunteers began to decrease. Recruitment emphasized skills.

May 5, 1969   At his first press conference, Director Blatchford mentioned that "(American college students) suspect the Peace Corps is almost lily-white–and they are right." He set up a special office for minority.

Jun., 1969   The first official act of Blatchford was to revise the Peace Corps Handbook and policies toward "individual responsibility." Changes included elimination of the book locker (books sent to volunteers), clothing allowance (for use after training, lowering free air freight for volunteer's baggage, restricting travel to Western Europe and the U.S.A., consolidating volunteer allowances into prorated monthly checks and permitting Country Directors to dismiss volunteers "for the convenience of the Peace Corps."

Jun. 30, 1969 Worldwide, volunteers totaled 12,131. According to the Peace Corps statistics, more than half of all volunteers (56%) who reported for training did not complete two years of service (attrition). Nearly one third of trainees did not complete training (31%). More than one third (37%) of those who were sworn in as volunteers either left voluntarily or were terminated prior to completion of service. Average volunteer age was 23.9 years. Volunteers included 67% men and 33% women.

Summer, 1969 Peace Corps returned to Guinea. A prestigious firm contracted to study Peace Corps Washington D.C. headquarters. The contract was later extended.

"Don't Think/Some Days" was produced in Honduras. The film is a documentary about the daily lives of five volunteers.

Aug. 31, 1969 Peace Corps Washington included the Office of the Director, Office of the Deputy Director, Office of General Counsel, Office of Public Affairs, Office of International and Special Programs, Office of Voluntary Action, Office of Medical Programs, Office of Volunteer Placement, Office of Administration, Office of Project Development, Evaluation & Research, Office of Training Support, Regional Offices and the new Office of Returned Peace Corps Volunteers Administrative expenses began to increase.

Sept. 1, 1969 A coup d'état took place in Libya. With a new military government, the Peace Corps program closed within 60 days. That same month, the Malawi congress passed a resolution requesting that Peace Corps volunteers be replaced within 18 months. Criticism of the Tanzania program included comments that the agency had never assimilated and that training was poor.

Oct. 15, 1969 On the first Vietnam Moratorium Day, more than 150 Peace Corps staff members marched 20 blocks in Washington D.C. to protest the Vietnam War. Many had taken annual leave and had flown in from overseas. Between 250 and 300 attended a speech given by Senator Frank Church (D-Idaho). He considered the protest patriotic: "the patriotism of Camus, who would have us love our country for what it ought to be." In other countries, groups of Peace Corps Volunteers held silent vigils. Some presented petitions to American ambassadors. Blatchford later responded to questions about volunteer's freedom of speech, "A fair hearing and due process will be guaranteed to all involved."

Fall, 1969 Twelve volunteers were fired for political activities.

The building which had housed Peace Corps and other government offices was renovated and cleared for exclusive Peace Corps use.

Dec., 1969 These programs opened: Guinea and Swaziland. This program closed: Libya.

These volunteers died during or immediately following service overseas: Patrick O'Reilly (El Salvador), Michael Kotzian (Colombia), Henry Shuler (India), Jeannette Stafford (Philippines), Sandra Smith (Bolivia), Susan Losikoff (Malaysia), and Henry Farrar (Afghanistan).

1970's: Reductions & Loss of Autonomy

1970

Jan. 6, 1970   Seven volunteers and two staff members in Afghanistan wore black armbands and read a statement of dissent about the Vietnam War at the U.S. Embassy hours before Vice President Spiro Agnew arrived.

Mar., 1970   The Modern Language Aptitude Test (to evaluate foreign language proficiency) was dropped from use.

May 9, 1970   Following a U.S. invasion of Cambodia, increased bombing of North Vietnam and the murder of four students by National Guardsmen in Ohio, volunteer dissent increased. Sixteen members of the Committee of Returned Volunteers (CRV) occupied the fourth floor Peace Corps offices in Washington D.C. Outside, other former volunteers picketed.

May 31, 1970   A powerful earthquake in northern Peru killed about 50,000 people including two Peace Corps volunteers. The town of Yungay was totally obliterated and buried as a giant avalanche sped down mountain slopes at the speed of sound. Less than 3,000 inhabitants of 41,000 survived. Only the top of the church steeple was visible.

Jun. 2, 1970   Volunteers in South Korea, Venezuela and Panama donated money so that two volunteers could travel to Washington D.C.

to meet with Director Blatchford and discuss volunteer opposition to the war.

Jun. 9, 1970   Director Joseph Blatchford arrived in Lima, Peru to coordinate U.S. assistance. Applications to join the Peace Corps decreased to 19,022 (less than half the number in 1966).

Jun. 30, 1970 Worldwide, volunteers totaled 9,513. The Committee of Returned Volunteers (CRV) called for abandonment of the Peace Corps: "We are the Marines in velvet gloves."

Jul., 1970   The Peace Corps re-authorization bill was signed into law which, among other things, permitted the agency to recruit and maintain volunteer families overseas beginning in 1971.

Nov., 1970   Top staff recalled and shredded an issue of *Volunteer* magazine which dealt with dissent. The editors were fired and the magazine reformatted.

Dec., 1970   According to the Peace Corps' adopted Cohort Method, the attrition rate (percent of volunteers who left service prior to completion) was at an all-time high of 55%. Psychiatric evaluation for placement was minimized. Trainees spent a few days at "conferences" prior to shipping overseas in order to decide whether they were meant to be volunteers. This was called "staging" The length of staging would vary over the coming years from 3 to 8 days.

This program opened: Democratic Republic of the Congo. These programs closed: Tanzania, the Somali Republic and Sri Lanka closed for a second time.

These volunteers died during or immediately following service overseas: Frederick Schwartz (Swaziland), Susan Davey, Marilyn McKay & Martha Merrill (Liberia), John Willis (Jamaica), David McCarthy and Joseph Nonnemacker (Micronesia), Judith Bosch (Iran), Gail Gross & Marie Clutterbuck (Peru), Daniel Jandorf

(Malaysia), Susan Rodgers & David Bogenschneider (Kenya) and Paul Overholtzer (Mauritius).

1971

Jan., 1971   The President's proposed budget included a 30% reduction in the Peace Corps budget, cutting the number of volunteers from 9,000 to 5,800.

Apr., 1971   The United Nations began to recruit volunteers for its own Peace Corps.

Jun. 30, 1971   Worldwide, volunteers totaled 7,066 serving in 55 countries. The number of volunteers had been reduced 42% within the first 30 months of the new administration.

Administrative expenses swelled to more one third of entire budget (36.9%). In 1966 (Shriver's last year) when a record 15,556 volunteers served, administrative expenses represented 20.9% of the budget. Blatchford's "New Directions" also had a significant impact upon who served. In 1971 community development volunteers (architects, engineers, surveyors, urban planners, community organizers & builders) decreased from nearly one quarter of all volunteers (in 1968) to 4.2%. While the relative numbers of teachers and health workers were stable, the relative number of volunteers in agriculture and "other" categories grew substantially.

The training center in Escondido, California was closed.

Peace Corps training was reduced to the original level–12 to 14 weeks.

These programs closed: Bolivia, Panama, and Guayana. The program in Mauritania reopened.

Returning volunteers complained that hundreds were sent overseas under-trained and ill-equipped to do their jobs. They also complained about poor medical and technical support.

Summer, 1971 The 10th anniversary issue of *Volunteer* newspaper was the last to be published.

Jul. 1, 1971   Kevin O'Donnell succeeded Joseph Blatchford as Director. O'Donnell was a former Peace Corps Country Director in Korea. Peace Corps joined other federal volunteer agencies (such as VISTA) in a new organization called ACTION. Sources since then have cited a desire to quietly euthanize the Peace Corps by allying it with a multitude of other agencies. Dwindling budgets would be less likely to engage the public if they were shrouded in a confusing bureaucratic mystery.

The Peace Corps was no longer an independent agency.

Dec. 17, 1971 Led by Congressman Otto Passman (D-Louisiana), Chair of a House Subcommittee on Foreign Aid Appropriations, Congress passed a resolution to drastically cut the proposed Peace Corps budget. The director ordered Peace Corps Washington to temporarily halt acceptance of new volunteers and to prepare plans for discharging volunteers in the event that the budget crisis was not resolved.

Dec., 1971   The U.S. Post Office issued a stamp to commemorate 10 years of Peace Corps service.

These programs opened: Mali, Mauritius, Mauritania and the Solomon Islands. These programs closed: Bolivia, Guyana, Panama, Guinea, and Nigeria.

These volunteers died during or immediately following service overseas: Ronald Kuhn (Sierra Leone), Kalman Hahn (Ghana), Philip Holland (India), Agatha Thornton, Valeria Roberts, Marsha Ragno, Michael Periard & James Henrietta (Liberia), Ann Kenney

(Micronesia), Richard Leahy (Ecuador), Robert Whitfield (Ghana), Terry Lawyer (Togo) and Linda Manke (Kenya).

1972

Mar. 7, 1972   Hours before a cable was to be sent terminating 2,313 volunteers in 33 countries, Congress restored the budget so that the Peace Corps could continue to operate at current levels.

Apr. 30, 1972 The Peace Corps began estimating (rather than recording) attrition rates. In 1972, it was estimated to be 47%.

Jun. 30, 1972   Worldwide, volunteers totaled 6,894, a 56% reduction from 1966. Adjusted for inflation, the budget was one third less than it had been in 1966.

Aug. 11, 1972   Donald Hess succeeded Kevin O'Donnell as Director. He increased the amount of in-country training. He championed a halt to cutting the number of volunteers.

Dec., 1972   These programs opened: Malta and Central African Republic. This program closed: Malawi.

These volunteers died during or immediately following service overseas: Craig Pollock, Robert Ritger & John Davidson (Ecuador), Dennis Ota (Togo), Alan C. Banner (W. Samoa), James Weeks (Mauritius), James Ryan (Ethiopia), Louis Morton (Uganda), William Challed (Iran), Paul Spratt (Zaire), Elizabeth Aldrich & William L. West (Kenya) and Robert Lillig (Nepal).

1973

Jun. 30, 1973 Worldwide, volunteers totaled 7,341 serving in 58 countries. Average volunteer age had risen to 27.2 years as had the relative portion of female volunteers to 36%. The number of applicants increased to 33,637. The Peace Corps began to recruit business volunteers. Worldwide, the relative number of teachers remained constant at nearly one half (48.4%). Likewise, health workers remained about constant at one in ten (8.8%). Community development and public works volunteers increased to more than one in ten (12.7%). The relative number of agriculture volunteers decreased to 22.3%. However, the creation of small fish ponds to increase protein intake was already underway and successful. The "other" category returned to earlier levels (4.5%) and business and public management represented 3.3% of all volunteers. This was in response to a House Foreign Affairs Committee Survey Team Report titled "Peace Corps in the 1970s." The report stressed two goals: to balance generalist and specialist somewhere between the extremes of the 1960's and the early 1970s; during the 1960's 70% of volunteers were generalists while in the early 1970's 70% were specialists. The second goal was to judge volunteer effectiveness in more qualitative terms for each volunteer.

Almost 85% of all trainees received training in their host country.

The Virgin Islands training center was closed.

Oct. 1, 1973   Nick Craw succeeded Donald Hess as Director. He wished to increase the number of volunteers and instituted several plans.

Dec., 1973   Peace Corps requested the aid of the National Academy of Sciences which set up a committee to review the agency's character, directions and activities.

These programs opened: Yemen Arab Republic, Kiribati, Gabon and Oman. These programs closed: Malawi and Uganda.

These volunteers died during or immediately following service overseas: Steven Messer (Costa Rica), Linda Fink (Zaire), Rene Courtway (Benin), Wilburn Johnson (Senegal), Gregory V. Baker (Dominican Republic), Roderic Turner (Ethiopia) and Linda Robinson (Niger).

1974

Jun. 30, 1974 Worldwide, volunteers totaled 8,044 serving in 68 countries, the largest number of nations to date. About 5% of all volunteers were older than 50 years.

The Puerto Rico center was closed.

Eleven volunteers served in India compared to 1,200 only a few years before.

Dec., 1974   These programs opened: Tuvalu, Bahrain, and Seychelles. These programs closed: Malta and Uruguay.

These volunteers died during or immediately following service overseas: Dennis Pfost (Peru), Bethanne Bahler (Jamaica), Denise Blake (Afghanistan), Denise Rosser (Cote d'Ivoire), Robert Parker & Curtis Jacoby (Dominican Republic) and Gerald Robillard (Zaire).

Dec. 31, 1974 The Privacy Act was passed. It required written consent from the individual prior to disclosure of his or her records except in a few exempted categories.

1975

Apr. 28, 1975 John Dellenback succeeded Nick Craw as Director. He placed great emphasis on recruiting generalists and worked to improve health care for volunteers.

Jun. 30, 1975 Worldwide, volunteers totaled 7,015. The ratio of male volunteers to female is fairly constant: two to one–63% male and 37% female.

During the fiscal year, the National Academy of Sciences submitted its report, including recommendations.

All training took place in-country or in a nearby country.

Dec., 1975   In response to the Percy Amendment passed by Congress in 1974 which mandated that American foreign aid devote more attention to women's concerns, the Peace Corps created the Women in Development Office.

This program opened: Rwanda. These programs closed: Peru and Mauritius.

These volunteers died during or immediately following service overseas: Robert Pastuszak (Cote d'Ivoire), Jacqueline Chezem (Costa Rica), Grace Russomanno & Diane Fahey (Liberia), Harold Summers & Barbara Christie (Benin), Cecil Perkins (E. Caribbean), Stephen Hamer (Malaysia), Roy Prior and Francis Gavit (Honduras), Thomas Cronin (Philippines) and H. Benjamin Gamber (Kenya).

1976

Jun. 30, 1976 Worldwide, volunteers totaled 5,958 serving in 56 countries. The number of volunteers had decreased 2,086 within a 24 month period to reach its lowest number since 1962.

Dec., 1976   No programs opened. These programs closed: Malawi, India and Iran.

These volunteers died during or immediately following service overseas: Thomas Carpenter (Sierra Leone), George Bradfield (Chile), James Hoffman & June Cross (Liberia), Charles Pinney (Malaysia), Stephen Malone (E. Caribbean), Rosanne Provini (Honduras), Paul Johnson (Guatemala), Robert Davis (Burkina Faso), Richard Mulvihill (Cameroon), Deborah Gardner (Tonga), Polly Zimmerman and Louise Wolf (Morocco).

1977

Feb. 14, 1977 A male volunteer was kidnapped in Colombia by a group known as FARC and held hostage for the next three years.

Jun. 30, 1977 Worldwide, volunteers totaled 5,752 serving in 56 countries. The number of applications decreased to 13,908 (nearly one quarter of those received in 1966). The relative number of women was increasing as the Peace Corps recruited more: 60.3% male and 39.7% female. The number of volunteers in community development decreased as emphasis was put on health/nutrition and food/water. The Peace Corps also changed its reporting methods for the type of work. Teachers were now called "knowledge and skills (program)" which constituted 44.4% of all volunteers. "The "health and nutrition (program)" included 16.6% of all volunteers, "food and water (program)" 17.1%. The "housing (program)", "energy and conservation (program)" and "community services (program) which might have once been called community development together included 12.9% of all volunteers. New emphasis was placed upon business and 9% of all volunteers were part of the "economic development and income (program)."

Likewise, an important change to management was made. Spouses were named as co-country directors, sharing a single salary for a two and one half year assignment.

Oct. 11, 1977 Carolyn R. Payton succeeded John Dellenback as Director. A staff member between 1964 and 1970, Payton was the first female and African-American to be appointed Director. She worked to recruit Americans of all ethnic and racial backgrounds.

Dec. 19, 1977 ACTION Update was first published.

Dec., 1977 By this time, Section 8(c) of the Peace Corps Act which required volunteer training about communism was totally ignored. "It was absolutely total bullshit," said Richard Sykes, Deputy Director.

No programs opened. These programs closed: Ethiopia and Venezuela.

These volunteers died during or immediately following service overseas: Gary Wilcox (Fiji) and Florence Krok (Kenya).

1978

Mar., 1978   One edition of *Peace Corps Times* was published as a "pilot program."

May 3, 1978   Peace Corps began anew to recruit "generalists." However, they were to be trained in specific skills like disease eradication, maternal & child health care, and agriculture. Up to 600 such assignments were being recruited for (10% of the worldwide effort). Even skilled volunteers were trained in specific techniques. For instance, someone who knew about farming might be trained in planting and storing grains in the Third World.

Jun. 30, 1978 Worldwide, volunteers totaled 7,072. The average volunteer age was 27.6 years. The proportion of male to female volunteers was constant: 61% male, 39% female. More seniors joined–8% of all volunteers were 60 years or older. The attrition rate in 1978 (43%) is the last time that it ever surpassed 40%.

Dec. 8, 1978   Minorities constituted 5.2% of all Peace Corps volunteers.

Dec., 1978   This program opened: Malawi. No programs closed.

These volunteers died during or immediately following service overseas: Lester Gliessman (Kenya), Jerry Bryan (Brazil), Christopher Luecke (Liberia), Richard Kelly (Belize), Robert Warren (Honduras), Christine Thompson (Ecuador), Robert Jonas (Colombia), Robert McFate (Chile), Dennis Stilson (E. Caribbean), Robert Benson and Debora White (Togo), Robert Owens (Morocco) and Eugene Galgas (Ghana).

1979

Jan. 23, 1979 ACTION identified eight programs for emphasis including: health and nutrition, food and water, knowledge and skills, economic development and income, community services, energy and conservation, housing and legal rights. Of these, the first three will be emphasized beginning in 1979. The goal was to have 80% of volunteers working in these areas within one year and 100% by 1980-1981. To achieve this goal, training was extended to 16 weeks of which six weeks were for "skills training" and ten weeks for "language training."

The number of volunteers involved in community services will be halved. Likewise the number of teachers will be reduced 21%. The number of volunteers involved with economic development & income will double.

Apr. 27, 1979 An amendment to ACTION legislation granting the Peace Corps special semi-independence was signed. Richard F. Celeste succeeded Carolyn R. Payton as Director. He invested energy in training, including a worldwide core curriculum. He was successful in involving increasing numbers of women and minorities, especially in staff.

Jun. 30, 1979 Worldwide, volunteers totaled 6,328.

Oct., 1979 Seventy volunteers recalled from El Salvador.

Dec. 22, 1979 A female volunteer was released by the February 28th Popular League in El Salvador after ten days in captivity. She returned home immediately.

Dec. 30, 1979 The National Council of Returned Peace Corps Volunteers was created (later renamed National Peace Corps Association).

During the year, pilot support systems were set up in the Pacific and Latin America to deal with stress and violence (including rape).

Another pilot program (CAST) involved lengthening "staging" (pre-service selection) to eight days.

Dec., 1979   This program reopened: Tanzania. These programs closed: Nicaragua, Chad, Afghanistan and Bahrain.

These volunteers died during or immediately following service overseas: Timothy Matthews (Sierra Leone) and Lois Ann Lane (Gambia).

1980's: Cooperation with Other Agencies

1980

Mar. 31, 1980 The program in El Salvador was closed.

Apr. 29, 1980 Seven couples served as co-country directors in Botswana, the Philippines, the Solomon Islands, Brazil, Morocco, the Eastern Caribbean and Guatemala.

Jun. 30, 1980 Worldwide, volunteers totaled 5,994 serving in 65 countries. Based upon the 1979 pilot program, training modules were sent over the planet as support mechanisms for volunteers suffering from stress or trauma. Likewise, the CAST model of lengthening "staging" to eight days was also used globally.

Since 1978,   110 volunteers were trained in warm water fisheries and placed in 17 nations. The attrition rate dropped to 37%, the lowest since 1964.

Summer, 1980 Many generalists attended technical skill training in one of these areas; fisheries, agro-forestry, vegetable cultivation, animal husbandry, alternative energy, rural water systems and primary health care. Afterwards, the volunteers were sent to their host country for ten weeks of language and cross-cultural training.

In Washington D.C., third year students from minority colleges worked as Peace Corps interns with the hope that they would soon join as volunteers.

Aug., 1980   The relative proportion of volunteers over 55 years of age decreased to 5%. In order to improve recruitment, articles appeared in such magazines as *McCalls* and *50 Plus*.

Sept., 1980   Recruiters ceased nominating for a specific job and place. They matched candidates with a general list of 40 job categories and places.

Oct. 14, 1980 Three thousand heard Senator Edmund Muskie (D-Maine), Robert Sargent Shriver Jr and Richard Celeste spoke at the University of Michigan, Ann Arbor to commemorate the 20th anniversary of JFK's impromptu, late-night speech to college students where he mentioned service abroad.

Dec., 1980   This program opened: Turks/Caicos Islands. This program closed: El Salvador.

These volunteers died during or immediately following service overseas: Thomas Lockhart (Sierra Leone), Lynne Masover (Fiji), Marian Baciewicz (Ghana), Mitchell Woodward (Ecuador), Thomas LeSuer (Lesotho), David Rubin (Micronesia) and Diana Fillmore (Gabon).

1981

Mar., 1981   The Peace Corps began a 15 city tour with conferences and seminars in commemoration of 20 years of service.

In response to budget cuts, a study began about streamlining headquarters in Washington, D.C. The CAST model for staging was briefly abandoned and the number of projected trainees decreased. Skill training, often taught in other countries, decreased.

May 7, 1981   Loret Miller Ruppe succeeded Richard F. Celeste as Director. She was the longest serving director who supported women's issues and promoted business-oriented projects. During her tenure the budget increased almost 50%, the number of volunteers by 20%, the average attrition rate decreased significantly and according to Senator Chris Dodd (D-Connecticut) "took the Peace Corps out of the pit of politics and made it non-partisan." Programs began or were renewed in 14 nations.

Jun. 1, 1981   In an interview, Director Ruppe pledged to coordinate the Peace Corps efforts with USAID.

Jun. 1981   As the final event of the 20th anniversary celebration, the Peace Corps sponsored a series of conferences and seminars in Washington D.C.

June. 30, 1981 Worldwide, volunteers totaled 5,445, a 10% decrease from the year before. As a pilot program, volunteers were assigned directly to private voluntary organizations in countries where the Peace Corps had no operational program.

Jul., 1981   During an attempted coup in Gambia, volunteers and staff members took refuge in the American Ambassador's compound for eight days as gun battles raged in the capital city. They were liberated by Senegalese commandos who explained that they liked Americans–their leader had been taught English years before by a volunteer.

Dec., 1981   Dean Coston Associates was contracted at the behest of Congress to produce a slide show about Marxism and the communist threat as part of volunteer training in accordance with Section 8(c) of the Peace Corps Act.

This program opened: Papua New Guinea. These programs closed: Colombia, Brazil, South Korea and Cote d'Ivoire.

These volunteers died during or immediately following service overseas: Theodore Cooper, Margaret Carmona and Daniel Greenwald

(Philippines), Harry Hushaw (Thailand), Philip Cyr & Marshal Haggard (Nepal), Brian Edens (Senegal), Janis Hyatt (Swaziland), John Marshall (Mali), Paul Chaljub (Chile), Jeanne Corbin & Darryl Adkins (Jamaica) and Bridgette McClellan (The Gambia).

1982

Feb. 22, 1982 Congress re-established the Peace Corps as an independent agency.

Jun. 30, 1982 Worldwide, volunteers totaled 5,380.

Dec., 1982 This program opened: the Cook Islands. These programs closed: Grenada and Chile.

This volunteer died during service overseas: Steven Presnal (Ecuador).

1983

May 7, 1983 *The Nation* magazine reported on a 1982 screening of the slide show about Marxism and the communist threat. Guatemala bound trainees viewed the show. Many claimed it was "negative, too simplistic and insulted our intelligence." Richard Abell, Special Assistant to the Director (and recent appointee) said, "I think that says something about the naiveté of the volunteers." The slide show was shelved.

Jun. 30, 1983 Worldwide, volunteers totaled 5,483.

Dec., 1983 The Peace Corps contributed 26 volunteers to the United Nations efforts, most of them working in countries which lacked a Peace Corps program. The nations included: China, Equatorial Guinea, Sao Tome e Principe, Somalia and Sudan.

Over the year, 350 volunteers were evacuated for medical reasons, three died from illness.

These programs opened: Sri Lanka, Haiti and Burundi. These programs closed: Oman and Malaysia.

These volunteers died during or immediately following service overseas: Robert Long (Liberia), Kimberly Morken (Botswana), Joseph Sheriff (Micronesia), Michael Wood (Guatemala), Kathryn Crotty (Mali), Diana Hess (Kenya), Terry Strong (Lesotho), Mark Edstrand (Niger) and James Wood (Togo).

A study of Peace Corps volunteer deaths between 1962 and 1983 reported that 70% of the 185 deaths involved motor vehicle accidents. However, between 1981 and 1983, suicide was the leading cause of death (13% of all volunteer deaths during that time period).

1984

Feb. 1, 1984   A new Small Enterprise Development Unit was established to offer generic training models and to increase business awareness to all volunteers. Volunteers were encouraged to tailor new businesses to local needs, acting as a liaison with other agencies when appropriate.

Jun., 1984   *Peace Corps Times* was published. The new format focused upon a country per issue.

Jun. 30, 1984   Worldwide, volunteers totaled 5,699 in 58 countries.

Sept., 1984   Five volunteers arrived in Sudan to assist in the new program.

Oct., 1984   Computers were installed in 21 country headquarter offices. More were planned for installation.

Nov. 23, 1984 The President of the Dominican Republic addressed all volunteers at a conference held there. Afterwards, he and the First Lady shook hands with and personally thanked each volunteer for his or her service.

Dec., 1984 The worldwide attrition rate decreased to 31%. It would remain near 30% for the remainder of the decade, averaging 32.6%.

These programs opened: Grenada and Sudan. No programs were closed.

These volunteers died during or immediately following service overseas: Shaun O'Brien & Charles Turneer (Philippines), Mark Streb (Niger), Jennifer Rubin (Togo), Ronald Cecchini (Thailand), William Mathis, Jr (Zaire), Peter Wolfe (Guatemala), Lesa Sanftleben (Lesotho) and William Schaffer (Nepal).

1985

Jan. 30, 1985 Teachers College/Columbia University offered scholarships to former volunteers willing to commit to 2 years of work as a teacher in the New York City public schools. This was called the Peace Corps Fellow Program.

Mar., 1985 During Peace Corps Week President Ronald Reagan hosted an event in the Rose Garden. "If we celebrated Volunteer Week every week, all year long," he said, "it wouldn't be enough time to honor all the remarkable, selfless Americans who give their time, money, labor and love to help their neighbors."

Jun.30, 1985 Worldwide, volunteers totaled 6,264 in 60 countries.

Oct. 21, 1985 Ann Arbor, Michigan began the 25th anniversary of the Peace Corps inception with conferences. Between this date and September, 1986, 25 cities hosted activities including Washington D.C.

Dec., 1985   Following efforts to improve coordination, 1,000 volunteer in 40 countries worked with USAID projects.

This program opened: Guinea. No programs closed.

These volunteers died during or immediately following service overseas; John Wright & Audrey Copeland (Ecuador), Raymond Kruger (Morocco) and Audrey Smith (Philippines).

1986

Feb., 1986   Volunteers were involved in increasing African food production. A large contingent of volunteers in the Americas worked to create income generation.

Jun. 30, 1986 Worldwide, volunteers totaled 5,913.

Aug., 1986   These nations issued Peace Corps stamps to commemorate 25 years of service: Tonga, the Solomon Islands, Tuvalu, Cameroon, Senegal, Sierra Leone and St. Lucia.

Sept.,1986   During the 25th anniversary celebration in Washington D.C. about 5,000 former volunteers gathered on the National Mall.

Dec., 1986   Agency work categories were food productivity, energy conservation, health, forestry, fisheries, small enterprise development, water resources, education, women in development and collaboration (with other agencies).

The Peace Corps released a 35 minute film titled "Let it Begin Here" for recruiting.

Congress approved the Higher Education Act of 1986 which included a provision for partial student loan forgiveness, available to VISTA and Peace Corps volunteers.

No programs opened. These programs closed: Sudan and the Cook Islands.

No volunteers died during service overseas.

1987

Jun. 30, 1987 Worldwide, volunteers totaled 5,219, the lowest number ever fielded.

Aug., 1987   The largest single contributor to the fisheries programs was USAID which provided transportation, materials, training, facilities and technical support in these nations: Central African Republic, Senegal, Cameroon, Zaire, Honduras, Jamaica, Guatemala, Philippines, Morocco and Thailand.

Dec., 1987   AIDS screening was introduced for all applicants.

These programs opened: Haiti and Burkina Faso. This program closed: Chad.

This volunteer died during service overseas: Joseph Teates (Guatemala).

1988

Jun. 30, 1988 Worldwide, volunteers totaled 5,812.

Dec., 1988   A volunteer in the Dominican Republic began the World Map Project, painting a world map on a large wall at a school. Other volunteers were taught and maps first spread across 100 public places in that country. Over the next decade, this example would be repeated across the globe.

These programs opened: the Cook Islands, Guinea Bissau, Cape Verde, Comoros, Equitorial Guinea and Pakistan. No programs closed.

These volunteers died during or immediately following service overseas: Scott Glotfelty (Togo), Danuta Kossowska (Thailand), Mathew Sherman (Honduras), Andrew Karrer (Micronesia), Brenda Crawford and Juanita Quiton (Swaziland) and Steven Butler (Tunisia).

1989

Jan. 31, 1989 The demographic make-up of volunteers changed radically over the years. By this date, more than half were women (52%). The average volunteer age was 30. 7.3% were over the age of 50 and 11% were married.

Jan., 1989 The National Peace Corps Association incorporated and began to publish a quarterly magazine.

Jan. 20, 1989 For the first time, volunteers and staff marched in the presidential inaugural parade.

Apr. 9-15, National Volunteer week.

1989

Apr., 1989 *RPCV Writers*, a quarterly, was published.

Apr. 20, 1989 Paul D. Coverdell succeeded Loret Miller Ruppe as Director. He established two programs of note. World Wise Schools was a means for American students to communicate with volunteers in an effort to meet the Peace Corps' third goal (see Appendix titled

"Peace Corps Goals). He announced that the agency would increase the number of volunteers in these areas: the environment, urban development and small enterprise development.

Volunteers and former volunteers wrote letters to students explaining what it was like in a foreign country. His other innovation was the Fellows/USA which assisted returning volunteers with graduate studies.

Jun. 30, 1989   Worldwide, volunteers totaled 6,248.

Aug., 1989   The Peace Corps Library (in Washington D.C.) included a librarian and a collection of books and materials related to Peace Corps history, languages, technical materials related to volunteer's work and information about countries served.

Dec., 1989   The *Peace Corps Times* printed an all-call to volunteers with journals. The Columbus and Company, Discover's Press announced that it sought journals for publication.

This program opened: Malta. No programs closed.

These volunteers died during or immediately following service overseas: Michelle Drabiski (Paraguay), Dorothy Osborne (Dominican Republic) and Margaret Schutzius (Chad).

1990's: Entrance into the Former Soviet Bloc

1990

Mar., 1990   The *Peace Corps Times* cut publication from six issues a year to four (quarterly).

Jun. 15, 1990   President George H. Bush hosted an event in the Rose garden just prior to the first Peace Corps volunteers' travel to the former

Soviet Bloc nations. He said, "The Peace Corps built its reputation the old-fashioned way, step by step, village by village, family by family, bringing the world a bit closer one friendship at a time."

Jun. 30, 1990 Worldwide, volunteers totaled 5,583. The attrition rate decreased to 29%, the lowest since 1961. Between 1990 and 1994, the average rate was 28.6%.

Dec., 1990 Emphasis on urban development was reinstituted.

These programs opened: Bolivia, Cote d'Ivoire, Namibia, Hungary, Poland, Vanuatu, and the Slovak Republic. The program in Chad was briefly closed, then reopened. These programs also closed: Liberia and the Philippines.

These volunteers died during or immediately following service overseas: Daniel Ohl (Kenya) and David Schaeffer (Tanzania).

1991

Jan. 15, 1991 As a result of the United Nations imposed deadline for the Iraqi withdrawal from Kuwait, volunteers were evacuated from Morocco, Tunisia, Pakistan, Mauritania, Tanzania and Yemen.

Mar. 1, 1991 A large cake was cut and speeches made at the Russell Senate Building in Washington D.C. to commemorate the 30th anniversary.

Jun., 1991 At a summit between the United States and Russia, Russian Foreign Minister Alexander Bessmertnykh said, "Don't insult us by mentioning the Peace Corps."

Jun. 30, 1991 Worldwide, volunteers totaled 5,866.

Jul., 1991 *RPCV Writers & Readers* was published bimonthly in an expanded format.

Aug. 1991   In Washington D.C., there were activities on the National Mall to celebrate the 30th anniversary.

Oct. 8, 1991   Elaine Chao succeeded Paul D. Coverdell as Director. The first Asian-American to serve as Director, she expanded programs to Eastern Europe and Central Asia following the disintegration of the Soviet Union.

Fall, 1991   Following rioting, 175 volunteers were evacuated from Democratic Republic of the Congo.

Dec., 1991   These programs opened: Nicaragua, Uruguay, Chile, Mauritania, Republic of Congo, Tunisia, Uganda, Zimbabwe, Bulgaria, Romania and Mongolia. These programs closed: Democratic Republic of the Congo, Mauritius, Tunisia, and Pakistan.

These volunteers died during or immediately following service overseas: David Edwards (Namibia) and Gloey Wiseman (Bolivia).

1992

Jun. 30, 1992   Worldwide, volunteers totaled 5,831.

Fall, 1992   Lotus Development Corporation donated Lotus 1-2-3 computer software for use in all Peace Corps headquarters around the globe.

Nov. 20, 1992 The first group of 100 volunteers was sent to Russia.

Dec., 1992   Acting Inspector General John S. Hale presented a 43 page report to Congress within which he warned of "a marked increase in violent acts against volunteers worldwide." He claimed that his warning was ignored.

These programs opened: Argentina, Nigeria, Albania, Estonia, Latvia, Lithuania, Russia, Ukraine, Armenia, Philippines, and Uzbekistan. Sierra Leone briefly closed then reopened.

These volunteers died during or immediately following service overseas: Susan Harding (Cote d'Ivoire), Varina Rogers (Malawi) and William Nordmann (Nepal).

1993

May 26, 1993 Since 1987 when the Peace Corps began to screen applicants for AIDS, 29 volunteers were reported HIV positive.

Jun. 12, 1993 The first group of volunteers (18 English teachers) arrived in China.

Jun. 30, 1993 Worldwide, volunteers totaled 6,467.

Summer, 1993 Peace Corps Times began publication of "Field Book" which included volunteer written installments about service. These included stories, poems, recipes, photos and observations.

Oct. 7, 1993 Carol Bellamy succeeded Elaine Chao as Director. She was the first former Peace Corps volunteer to be confirmed by the Senate as Peace Corps Director.

Fall, 1993 The Peace Corps began to install country headquarters with equipment to connect to the Internet.

Dec., 1993 These programs opened: El Salvador, Madagascar, Zambia, Moldova, China, Kazakhstan, Kyrgyz Republic, and Turkmenistan. These programs closed: Burundi Equitorial Guinea and Rwanda.

These volunteers died during or immediately following service overseas: Mary Johnson (China), Karren Wald (Togo), Michele Sylvester (Senegal) and Layne Pfaffenberger (Guatemala).

1994

Jun. 30, 1994 Worldwide, volunteers totaled 6,745.

Dec., 1994 The number of applications (13,628) was almost the same as the number received in 1977, about one quarter of those received in 1966. The relative numbers of volunteers worked in these areas: 40% in education, 18% in agriculture, 13% in the environment and forestry, 17% in health, 9% in business and 3% in urban planning. Ethnic minorities represented 12% of all volunteers. More than half of the volunteers were women (53%). The average volunteer age had risen to 31 years with 8% over 50 years of age.

Most training lasted 12 to 14 weeks.

As part of the Women in Development program, gender and development training workshops began in Central and South America.

This program opened: Niue. These programs closed: Argentina, Sierra Leone and Yemen.

This volunteer died during service overseas: Thomas Barakatt (W. Samoa).

1995

Spring, 1995 Worldwide, 90% of country headquarters were connected to the Internet.

Jun. 30, 1995   Worldwide, volunteers totaled 7,218.

Jul., 1995   The Peace Corps released a new 15 minute recruiting film titled "What is a Peace Corps Volunteer" which targeted grades 3 through 12.

Aug.11, 1995   Mark D. Gearan succeeded Carol Bellamy as Director. He established the Crisis Corps which still places former volunteers in areas beset by natural and humanitarian disasters for a limited time period.

Dec., 1995   These programs opened: Guyana, Suriname, Burkina Faso, Eritrea, and Ethiopia. These programs closed: Comoros, Nigeria and the Cook Islands.

These volunteers died during or immediately following service overseas; Lucille Raimondo (Guatemala), Donald Weber (Hungary), Andrew Shippee (Cameroon) and Jeffrey Orton (Niger).

1996

Apr. 5, 1996   Since its inception in 1989, World Wise Schools had communicated with 300,000 American students in 50 states, explaining what it was like in a foreign country. The Peace Corps Fellows Program now included 26 colleges and universities from which former Peace Corps Volunteers had acquired masters' degrees with scholarships and/or reduced tuition in exchange for a two year commitment to teach or work in local social projects.

Jun. 30, 1996   Worldwide, volunteers totaled 6,910.

Dec., 1996   While visiting Asunción, Paraguay, First Lady Hillary Rodham Clinton said, "For nearly 35 years the Peace Corps have represented the United States' commitment to social investment. It does not often receive the headlines that political action or economic progress does, but underneath both is the steady work done by Peace

Corps Volunteers in partnership with the citizens of the countries in which they serve."

As an ongoing part of the Women in Development program, gender and development training pilot workshops began in Africa.

Peace Corps Crossroads was published online.

In countries around the globe, volunteers began to use the radio for education, entertainment and business models. In many cases they had their own programs.

The Crisis Corps began. Former volunteers were sent to nations on a short-term basis, primarily to aid in reconstruction after a natural disaster.

As assaults on volunteers increased, the number of medical evacuations for stress-related problems also increased by 78%. Dr. Joan P. Gerring believed that there was a correlation between volunteer safety and mental health.

Worldwide attrition increased to one third (the early 1960's level).

No programs opened. These programs closed: Central African Republic, Chad, Seychelles, Swaziland, Tunisia and the Marshall Islands.

These volunteers died during or immediately following service overseas: Laura Stedman (Swaziland), Nancy Coutu (Madagascar), Robert Lindstrom (Poland), Annika Rodriguez (Honduras) and Kyrstin Scharninghausen (Namibia).

1997

Feb. 14, 1997 The first group of 32 trainees arrived in Johannesburg, South Africa.

Jun. 30, 1997   Worldwide, volunteers totaled 6,660.

Dec., 1997   Volunteers posted messages on the Internet from foreign countries. For the first time, their daily lives were instantaneously in the public domain.

These programs opened; South Africa and Jordan. These programs closed: Uruguay, Botswana, Republic of the Congo, Albania, Czech Republic, Hungary, and Tuvalu.

These volunteers died during or immediately following service overseas: Jeremy Rolfs (Lesotho), Elizabeth Livingston (Costa Rica), Jeremiah Mack (Niger) and Chad Nettesheim (Dominican Republic).

Between 1961 and 1997, 74% of all fatalities were caused by accidents, and most of these by motor vehicle accidents.

1998

Feb. 6, 1998   The relative number of volunteers worked in these areas: education 37%, health 18%, environment 18%, business 13%, agriculture 9% and other 5%. Volunteers 50 years or older represented 6% and overall, women constituted more than half of all volunteers (58%). Ethnic minority volunteers represented 13% of the Peace Corps.

Jun. 30, 1998   Worldwide, volunteers totaled 6,719.

Dec., 1998   As implied by Dr. Joan P. Gerring, attrition rates began to increase. The Peace Corps application became electronic.

The Crisis Corps had involved 90 former volunteers in 13 nations since its inception in 1996.

This program opened; Mozambique. These programs closed: Chile, Eritrea, Guinea Bissau, Malta, Sri Lanka, and Fiji.

These volunteers died during or immediately following service overseas: Kevin Leveille (Cote d'Ivoire), Joie Kallison (Namibia), Timothy Simpson (Nepal), Robert Bock (Philippines), Etienne Victor Verloo (Ukraine), Kathryn MacGillivary (Malawi) and Karen Phillips (Gabon).

1999

Jun. 30, 1999   The U.S. Postal service announced a new Peace Corps stamp which was based upon a replica of a Norman Rockwell painting.

Worldwide, volunteers totaled 6,989.

Dec. 23, 1999 Mark L. Schneider succeeded Mark D. Gearan as Director. He was the second former volunteer confirmed by the Senate. He campaigned to increase a volunteer contribution to fighting HIV/AIDS in Africa and also recruited volunteers with computer backgrounds to enhance foreign potential.

Dec. 1999   *Peace Corps Writers* was published bimonthly online. Eventually this would include a Peace Corps bibliography.

No programs opened. These programs closed: Ethiopia and Uganda.

These volunteers died during or immediately following service overseas: Helene Hill (Namibia) and Brian Krow (Ukraine).

2000's: New Communications & HIV/AIDS

2000

Mar. 7, 2000   As part of the World Wise Schools, 43 volunteers telephoned American classrooms on Peace Corps Day from their foreign posts. They spoke with students for 30 minutes about their lives in a foreign country.

Jun. 28, 2000 2,400 volunteers in Africa began teaching HIV/AIDS prevention.

Jun. 30, 2000 Worldwide, volunteers totaled 7,164.

Dec., 2000 These programs opened: Uganda and Herzegovina. This program closed; Solomon Islands.

These volunteers died during or immediately following service overseas: Justin Bhansali & Jesse Thyne (Guinea), William DiDiego (Cote d'Ivoire), Judith Pasmore (Lesotho) and Jennifer Rose (Malawi).

2001

Jun. 30, 2001 Worldwide, volunteers totaled 6,643.

Jul., 2001 *Peace Corps Online* was published online. This included an electronic library of Peace Corps documents.

Sept. 7, 2001 The Peace Corps Manual was revised, limiting motorcycle use to those volunteers who needed it for their assignment (project-by-project basis). Any volunteer who did not wish to drive a motorcycle was given another assignment with alternative transportation. Those who chose to use the provided motorcycle were tutored in its operation during training, given a helmet and tools.

Sept. 14, 2001 Following attacks on New York and Washington D.C. by extremists from the Middle East using commercial jets, the National Peace Corps Association cancelled its Washington D.C. conference originally scheduled for Sept. 22 to commemorate the 40th anniversary.

Nov. 10, 2001 "I'm not defending the old Peace Corps," said Robert Sargent Shriver Jr during a speech at Yale University, "I'm attacking it! We didn't go far enough! ...We never really gave the goal of 'World Wide Peace' an overwhelming commitment." He went on to suggest a new fourth goal; to bind all human beings together in a common cause to assure peace and survival for all.

Dec., 2001   Increased volunteer use of computers sparked concerns for their safety. An official memorandum was sent worldwide to warn volunteers against disclosing their precise living location or personal possessions.

The Peace Corps Times ceased publication.

This program opened: Georgia. These programs closed: Poland and Papua New Guinea.

These volunteers died during or immediately following service overseas: Natalie Waldinger and Wyatt Pillsbury (Tanzania), Carlos Amador (El Salvador), Jang Lee (Uzbekistan), Larisa Jaffe (Zimbabwe), Susan Fagan (Ghana) and Ronald G. Mc Dearman (Kenya). This volunteer was missing: Walter J. Poirier (Kenya).

2002

Jan.23, 2002 A group of former volunteers and former directors opposed the latest Director's nomination and spoke at the Senate Foreign Relations Committee nomination hearings. For the first time, there was dissent with a final Committee vote of 14 to 4 to recommend confirmation to the Senate.

Gaddi H. Vasquez succeeded Mark L. Schneider as Director. The first Hispanic Director, he recruited from more ethnic and racial groups, opened a program in Mexico, enhanced security and safety programs and initiated the President's Emergency Plan for AIDS Relief. During his tenure the number of volunteers increased by 15%.

Jun. 30, 2002 Worldwide, volunteers totaled 6,636.

Jul., 2002 A G.A.O. report recommended that the Peace Corps propose modifications to the Peace Corps Act permitting security personnel to be employed more than five years.

Oct. 12, 2002 Former volunteers joined an anti-war march in Hancock, Michigan.

Nov. 4, 2002 Anti-war protestors, including former volunteers, were arrested for criminal trespass outside of Senator Zell Miller's office (R-Georgia) in Atlanta, Georgia.

Dec., 2002 Assault on Peace Corps volunteers increased 125% between 1991 and 2002 although the number of volunteers only increased 29%. More than half involved female volunteers, alone.

In 2002, the first Peace Corps memoirs were published using Print On Demand. Although Print On Demand had been experimented with since the mid-1990's, in 2002 companies began to produce full length books, one at a time, totally based upon electronic formats. Other types of printing required a professional to physically prepare a book for printing. Electronic formatting meant that once typed, the document was ready and a paper transfer was not necessary. One sent the books electronically. Instead of taking months, printing now took days. For self-publishing authors, the print set-up was a mere few hundred dollars instead of eight to ten times that amount for a limited run of 500 books.

These programs opened: Peru and East Timor. These programs closed: Zimbabwe, Herzegovina, Latvia, Lithuania, Slovak Republic, Jordan, and Niue.

This volunteer died during service oversea: Elizabeth Bowers (Zambia).

2003

Feb. 21, 2003 The NY Times ran a half page advertisement in opposition to the war in Iraq. This was funded by former volunteers.

Mar. 5, 2003 During a protest march involving about 100 anti-war demonstrators on the National Mall in Washington D.C., a former volunteer was arrested for his failure to remove a t-shirt that read "Peace on Earth." The charge against him was criminal trespass.

Mar. 14, 2003 The NY Times ran a second half page advertisement in opposition to the war in Iraq. This was also funded by former volunteers.

Mar. 31, 2003 A group of 60 to 70 volunteers in the Dominican Republic planned an anti-Iraq War protest to be held outside the American Embassy in Santo Domingo. Three days before the protest, volunteers were warned that they could be fired. Three volunteers participated. No action was taken against them.

May, 2003 As part of recently enacted legislation which directed $15 billion over the next five years to fight HIV/AIDS, tuberculosis and malaria, the Peace Corps committed an additional 1,000 volunteers to work in the Caribbean and in Africa.

Jun. 30, 2003 Worldwide, volunteers totaled 7,533.

Aug. 12, 2003 A former volunteer was fined $10,000 for traveling to Iraq in protest to the war. Part of about 300 protestors from around the globe who camped out near suspected American bombing targets (the human shield), the volunteer spent three weeks in Iraq working with children.

Sept. 30, 2003 Congress passed a Consolidated Appropriations Bill which exempted certain Peace Corps security and safety related positions from the five year employment limit rule.

Fall, 2003   The Dayton Daily News ran a week-long series of articles about increasing violence against volunteers overseas. Nearly three-quarters of the victims were female volunteers. Rape was of particular concern. Since 1991, violence against volunteers had doubled.

Dec., 2003   These programs opened: Botswana, Chad, Swaziland, Albania and Azerbaijan. These programs closed: Cote d'Ivoire and Russia.

This volunteer died during service overseas: Zack Merrill (Mali).

2004

Jan., 2004   The National Peace Corps Association began to publish an e-magazine.

Jan. 23, 2004 The President signed into law a Consolidated Appropriations Bill which exempted certain security and safety related Peace Corps positions from the five year limit to employment.

Mar. 24, 2004 Congress held hearings on world-wide increased violence against Peace Corps volunteers. While Gaddi Vasquez, Director, defended the agency's response, other witnesses disagreed. Jeffrey Bruce, editor of the Dayton Daily News said, "The extent of this safety problem has been disguised for decades, partly because the assaults occurred thousands of miles away, partly because the Peace Corps has made little effort to publicize them, and partly because the agency deliberately kept people from finding out while emphasizing the positive aspects of Peace Corps service." The father of Walter J. Poirier, missing in Bolivia since 2001, was blunter, "We found Peace Corps to be more concerned with its image and protecting the aura and prestige of the Peace Corps than any other issue."

Jun. 1, 2004   *American Taboo; A Murder in the Peace Corps* was published. This book describes the murder of a female volunteer on the island of Tonga in 1976. Later, it was the subject of a television show.

Jun. 30, 2004 Worldwide, volunteers totaled 7,733. The annual Peace Corps security and safety report stated that 23 security and safety related staff positions had been exempted from the five year limit to employment.

Nov. 4, 2004 "Jimi Sir," a movie about being a Peace Corps Volunteer, premiered in Belmont, Massachusetts at the Belmont Studio Cinema.

Dec., 2004 These programs opened: Mexico and Jordan. No programs closed.

These volunteers died during or immediately following service overseas: Gregor V. Baker (Ecuador), Melissa Mosvick (Morocco) and Rick Weiss (Philippines).

2005

Feb., 2005 YouTube, an internet based company, was created. Anyone could post films which were then viewed as part of the public domain. Peace Corps volunteers began to post documentaries about their lives almost immediately.

Jun. 30, 2005 Worldwide, volunteers totaled 7,810.

Nov., 2005 *Peace Corps Writers* (online) incorporated a daily blog about Peace Corps experiences.

Dec., 2005 No programs opened. These programs closed: Gabon, Nepal and Uzbekistan.

These volunteers died during or immediately following service overseas: Wyatt Ammon (Zambia) and Patricia Scataloni (Macedonia).

2006

Jun. 30, 2006 The Crisis Corps sent 130 former volunteers to the American Gulf Coast to aid in reconstruction following Hurricanes Katrina and Rita in 2005. This was the first time that the Crisis Corps was used domestically. It also sent 21 former volunteers to Southeast Asia for relief following a tsunami.

Worldwide, volunteers totaled 7,628.

Aug., 2006 Volunteer "blog sites" on the Internet numbered 1,300.

Sept. 26, 2006 Ronald A. Tschetter succeeded Gaddi H. Vasquez as Director. A former volunteer, he recruited more volunteers over the age of 50 and promoted volunteerism.

Fall, 2006 Foreign headquarters included one computer work station for every 25 volunteers.

Dec., 2006 The attrition rate increased to 35%, the highest since the first Gulf War.

More than half of all volunteers reported working against the HIV/AIDS epidemic (55%).

This program opened: Cambodia. These programs closed: Chad, Bangladesh and East Timor.

These volunteers died during or immediately following service overseas: Tessa Horan (Tonga), Justin Brady and Matthew Costa (Mali).

2007

Jun. 30, 2007 Worldwide, volunteers totaled 7,896.

Fall, 2007   More than half of all volunteers were women (59%). This is a reverse of the trend during the 1960's when men represented 65%. The relative number of ethnic minority volunteers had risen to 17% of the total while those over the age of 50 represented 5%. During the 1960's some estimated that less than 1% of volunteers were ethnic minorities. The average volunteer age decreased to 27 years (three and one half years older than those volunteers who served in 1965).

Nov., 2007   Assistant Regional Security Officer Vincent Cooper reportedly told a group of volunteers and at least one Fulbright Scholar to "keep tabs" on the Cubans and Venezuelans in Bolivia.

Dec., 2007   In its annual report on safety, the Peace Corps documented nearly 100 cases of sexual assault per year for 2006 and 2007. Victims were 92% women, mostly very young (20's) and alone.

The number of Peace Corps memoirs published increased dramatically due to Print On Demand's lower costs and easier set-up.

Fort Collins, Colorado (former home to the Colorado State University Research Foundation) formed an ad hoc committee to solicit donations for the construction of a three-story Peace Corps Museum.

This program reopened: Ethiopia. No programs closed.

These volunteers died during or immediately following service overseas: Julia Campbell (Philippines), Marilyn Foss (China), John Douglas Roberts (Vanuatu) and Blythe Ann O'Sullivan (Suriname).

2008

Jan., 2008   A volunteer in the Ukraine tested HIV positive after 13 months service. He was fired and sent home.

Feb., 2008   International news affiliates reported the November, 2007 incident which was corroborated by the U.S. Embassy as a mistake. The security officer was reportedly removed from the country. After the Bolivian President declared the U.S. Ambassador a persona non-grata, he returned to Washington D.C. The Peace Corps reiterated its policy against volunteer espionage.

Apr., 2008   The ACLU, representing the HIV positive volunteer, sent a letter to the Peace Corps within which it cited court decisions and reminded the agency that it could not discriminate against volunteers merely because they tested positive during service.

Apr. 15, 2008 A study of Peace Corps volunteer deaths between 1984 and 2003 concluded that the death rate had decreased compared to the rate between 1962 and 1983. However, while the number of accidents and suicides had decreased, the number of homicides had increased.

June, 2008   *Peace Corps Writers* posted an electronic bibliography of all known former volunteers' books.

Jun. 30, 2008 Worldwide, volunteers totaled 7,876.

Jul. 31, 2008 Peace Corps announced a new policy that it would not automatically end an HIV positive volunteer's employment.

Aug. 22,2008 Fort Collins, Colorado and the Colorado Returned Peace Corps Volunteers held a three day reunion and conference at the Northside Aztlan Community Center. Hundreds participated.

Fall, 2008   All "Letters to the Editor" in *Peace Corps Times* (by volunteers overseas) were electronic.

Nov. 14, 2008 During the last ten years, volunteers have been evacuated from at least 27 countries. At least three evacuations were directly attributed by the Congressional Research Service to the War on Terror; Uzbekistan, Turkmenistan and Kyrgyz Republic.

Dec., 2008   Volunteer "blog sites" on the Internet numbered 5,000. The number had nearly quadrupled within 28 months, primarily due to the popularity of lap-top computers.

These programs reopened: Liberia and Rwanda. This program closed: Kiribati.

These volunteers died during or immediately following service overseas: Catherine Saltwick (Botswana) and Bertie Lee Murphy (Belize).

2009

Jan., 2009   *Peace Corps Worldwide*, an online blog site, replaced *Peace Corps Writers.*

Jun. 22, 2009 Former volunteers began a letter-writing campaign to establish a Peace Corps Experience Special Collection at the Library of Congress. Based upon donations, the collection could include all published materials by former volunteers and staff.

Jun. 30, 2009 Worldwide, volunteers totaled 7,671. Applications totaled 15,386, about one third of the number that applied in 1966 although the population had doubled since then.

Former volunteers were publishing about five books per month about their experiences. The majority (90%) of these books were published at the author's expense using Print On Demand technology which permitted the publication of one book at a time. In the U.S.A., Print On Demand titles published outnumbered those printed by traditional commercial publishing houses.

Aug. 7, 2009   Aaron S. Williams succeeded Ronald A. Tschetter as Director. He was the fourth former volunteer to serve as Director.

Nov. 16, 2009 Nearly seven years after the Dayton Daily News reported about dangers for volunteers, the 2009 Peace Corps

Performance and Accountability Report stated that only 21% of foreign posts had annual reviews of safety and security plans. Only one in four performance goals to enhance volunteer safety and security had been met.

Nov., 2009   Two films by former volunteers were screened in Columbus, Missouri at the 4th annual Third Goal International Film Festival. They included "Gone to Mali" and "Once in Afghanistan"

Dec. 16, 2009 The Consolidated Appropriations Act, 2010 provided for the largest Peace Corps funding increase in more than a decade ($60 million). It also mandated that the director prepare and present a comprehensive assessment of the agency.

Dec., 2009   No programs opened. This program closed: Guinea. This program was suspended: Mauritania.

These volunteers died during or immediately following service overseas: Catherine Puzey (Benin), Joseph Chow (Tanzania) and So-Youn Kim (Morocco).

Peace Corps officials transferred oversight of violent crime to the safety and security office.

Dec. 31, 2009 The Peace Corps announced the founding of a digital library to include materials from 1961 to 2010: donated photos and stories by former volunteers, newsletters, speeches, annual reports, brochures, posters audio and video clips. "Our resources do not permit us to serve as a comprehensive Peace Corps historic archive, nor is it our mandate to do so," stated the agency on their website.

2010

Mar. 1, 2010   The Peace Corps sponsored 140 recruiting events to celebrate the 49th year of existence.

Mar. 29, 2010 Critically acclaimed *South of the Frontera: A Peace Corps Memoir* published.

Apr. 15, 2010 First Response Action, a group of former volunteers who survived sexual assault, posted a web site about their efforts to convince the Peace Corps to adopt a Seven-Point Plan for improving reaction to rape. In response to a letter that the leader of the group sent to Director Aaron Williams, two staff members made a conference call to her during which they reported the agency's support.

Apr., 2010 The annual safety and security report was released. Although sexual assault on volunteers (rape and attempted rape) had more than doubled since the 1990s, recommendations did not include serious prevention (training and equipment). Instead, the report recommended more studies, reports, classes for volunteers on "life-style" and even required that trainees sign statements that they understood "inherent risks." No mention was made that nearly 4 in 10 volunteers had served in Africa which had the highest HIV/AIDS rate in the world.

Spring, 2010 Volunteers continued to use the World Map Project model, begun in 1988. World maps, painted in public places, existed on five continents.

Electronic books (paperless) represented 8% of all books published in the U.S.A. Many of these were Peace Corps volunteer memoirs about their experiences. Nearly 1,000 volunteers had returned home to write at least one book (one author for every 200 volunteers).

Jun. 1, 2010 More than 5,000 films had been posted on YouTube by Peace Corps volunteers around the globe. More than one half million checked Volunteer blog sites and/or about the Peace Corps.

Jun. 16, 2010 The director presented a 200 page report to Congress concerning the requested agency assessment. The report recommended that the "5 year rule," revised in 2003 with exceptions, be further relaxed. The report also stated that headquarters (Washington D.C.) employed 536 to support an estimated 7,800 volunteers in 77 nations.

The last time the Peace Corps fielded a comparable number of volunteers was in 1974 when about 8,000 served in 68 nations. That year they were supported by 156 employees in Washington D.C. Although the headquarters support staff had more than tripled and communications became instantaneous with computers, the time of application to invitation had increased to 15.5 months, training of volunteers was reduced from 12 to 14 weeks to 10 to 12 weeks and as mentioned earlier, no appropriate rape prevention had been undertaken. Note that training had included 16 to 17 weeks in 1967. The same report stated that 23 programs had been closed or suspended within the past decade. Seventeen were related to "serious concerns for volunteer safety."

Jun. 23, 2010 Rep. Barbara Lee (D-CA) introduced legislation to issue a semi-annual Peace Corps stamp which would cost slightly more than required. Extra funds would be directed to the Peace Corps.

Jun. 30, 2010 A House subcommittee approved an 11.5% increase in the Peace Corps budget for the fiscal year 2011-2012. If approved by Congress (along with the annual budget request), this would be the second highest annual increase in agency history, the highest being approved in 2009. Amidst budget cuts, the Peace Corps was an exception.

Summer, 2010 The Peace Corps Fellows program included 50 colleges and universities from which former Peace Corps Volunteers had acquired masters' degrees with scholarships and/or reduced tuition in exchange for a two year commitment to teach or work in local social projects. Initially created in 1985 to prepare former volunteers as teachers in New York City public schools, the project has resulted in 556 teachers in that system to date.

Sept., 2010 The House of Representatives passed the proposed increase to funding.

Oct. 11-15, 2010 The University of Michigan sponsored a series of activities to celebrate the 50th anniversary of JFK's speech on the steps of the Michigan Union building.

Dec., 2010   These programs reopened: Colombia, Indonesia and Sierra Leone.

These volunteers died during or immediately following service overseas: Thomas Maresco (Lestho) and Stephanie Chance (Niger).

SOURCES

books

_____. *The Great Adventure.* Peace Corps, 1997.

_____. *At Home in the World: The Peace Corps Story.* Peace Corps, 1996.

Birky-Kreutzer, Pauline. *Peace Corps Pioneer or 'The Perils of Pauline'.* Prairie Publications: Urbana, Il, 2003.

Cobbs Hoffman, Elizabeth. *All You Need Is Love: The Peace Corps and the Spirit of the 1960's.* Harvard U. Press: Cambridge, MA, 1998.

Searles, David P.. *The Peace Corps Experience: Challenge and Change, 1969-1976.* University Press of Kentucky: Lexington, KY, 1997.

Sherman, John. *War Stories; A Memoir of Nigeria and Biafra.* Mesa Verde Press: Indianapolis, IN, 2002.

Smith, Robin McCollough. *A History of the Training Selection Process in the United States Peace Corps (Training).* Education D., Indiana University, 1985, AAT 8520487.

magazines/newspapers

_____. "The Box Score," *Peace Corps News.* Public Information Division: WA DC, Feb. 1962, p 2.

_____. "A Pleasant View...," *Peace Corps News.* Public Information Division: WA DC, March, 1962, p 2.

_____. "The Box Score." *Peace Corps New.* Public Information Division: WA DC, Vol. 2, No. 5, June, 1962, p 6.

_____."Peace Corps Around the World." *Peace Corps Volunteer:* WA DC, Vol. 1, No. 2, Dec., 1962, p 4.

_____. "Corps Now in 46 Countries." *Peace Corps News:* A Special College Supplement, WA DC, Vol. 2, No. 3, Fall, 1964, p 2.

_____. "Volunteers Ply Many Trades." *Peace Corps News:* Public Information Division, WA DC, summer, 1965, end page.

_____. "Some facts and figures." *Peace Corps Volunteer:* WA DC, Vol. V, No. 4, Feb., 1967, p 19.

_____. "New Stamps." *Peace Corps Volunteer:* WA DC, Vol. VII, No. 5, Mar., 1968, p 11.

_____. "U.N. to study volunteer corps." *Peace Corps Volunteer:* WA DC, Vol. VII, No. 4, Mar., 1969, p 22.

_____. "New Policies untie some apron strings." *Peace Corps Volunteer:* WA DC, Vol. VII, No. 8, Jul., 1969, p 7.

_____. "In Washington: New structure off drawing boards." *Peace Corps Volunteer:* WA DC, Vol. VII, No. 12, Nov., 1969, p 25-27.

_____. "Volunteers join moratorium with petitions, vigils." *Peace Corps Volunteer:* WA DC, Vol. VII, No. 13, Dec., 1969, p 2.

_____. "Libya pulls the plug on 'model' program." *Peace Corps Volunteer:* WA DC, Vol. VII, No. 13, Dec., 1969, p 3.

_____. "In Malawi bad news from Banda..." *Peace Corps Volunteer:* WA DC, Vol. VII, No. 13, Dec., 1969, p 4.

_____. "Protest In Afghanistan: A Case Study." *Peace Corps Volunteer:* WA DC, Vol. VIII, No. 3 & 4, Mar.-Apr., 1970, p 13.

_____. "News: MLAT." *Peace Corps Volunteer:* WA DC, Vol. VIII, No. 3 & 4, Mar.-Apr., 1970, p 20.

_____. "News: Peru." *Peace Corps Volunteer:* WA DC, Vol. VII, No. 5 & 6, May-Jun., 1970, p 16.

_____. "Peace, Politics and Blatchford." *Peace Corps Volunteer:* WA DC, Vol. VII, No. 5 & 6, May-Jun., 1970, p 19-20.

_____. "News: Congress." *Peace Corps Volunteer:* WA DC, Vol. VIII, No. 7 & 8, Jul.-Aug., 1970, p 25.

_____, "New Directions in Recruiting." *ACTION Update:* WA DC, May 3, 1978, p 13-14.

_____, "Peace Corps Times." *ACTION Update:* WA DC, May 3, 1978, p 12.

_____. "Peace Corps Profiles." *ACTION Update:* WA DC, Jun. 9, 1978, p 6.

_____. "Minority Recruitment Committee Presents Recommendations to Agency Director," *ACTION Update:* WA DC, Dec. 8, 1978, p 4.

_____. "Why Critics Lambaste San Brown's Agency." *U.S. News & World Report:* 86:37, Jan. 15, 1979.

_____. "PCV Held Hostage in El Salvador Has Fond Memories of Her Assignment." *ACTION Update:* WA DC, Feb. 29, 1980, p 6.

_____. "PC Multi-Country Training Will Enhance Volunteer Flexibility." *ACTION Update:* WA DC, Feb. 29, 1980, p 9.

_____. "Peace Corps Country Co-Directors Provide Dual Talents and Energy." *ACTION Update:* WA DC, Apr. 29, 1980, p 6.

_____. "Program to Increase Awareness, Involvement in PC Issues." *ACTION Update:* WA DC, May 21, 1980, p 2.

_____. "PC Plans Return of Volunteers to Nicaragua in August." *ACTION Update:* WA DC, Jun. 11, 1980, p 5.

_____. "PC Develops Improved Candidate Placement System." *ACTION Update:* WA DC, Aug. 27, 1980, p 3.

_____. "Peace Corps Kicks-off 20th Anniversary Celebration," *ACTION Update:* WA DC, Sept. 19, 1980, p 6.

_____. "Muskie Speaks at Ann Arbor Event." *ACTION Update:* WA DC, Oct. 30, 1980, p 1-2.

_____, "ACTION/Peace Corps Directors Discuss Their Administrations." *ACTION Update:* WA DC, Jan. 15, 1981, p 8.

_____, "Peace Corps 20th Anniversary Event to Begin Nationwide." *ACTION Update:* WA DC, Feb. 5, 1981, p 4.

_____."Senate Confirms Ruppe as PC Director." *ACTION Update:* WA DC, Jun. 1, 1981, p 6.

_____. "To Your Health: An Ounce of Prevention." *Peace Corps Times:* WA DC, Sept.-Oct., 1984, p 3.

_____. "Welcome to the Overseas Computer System." *Peace Corps Times:* WA DC, Sept.-Oct., 1984, p 12.

_____. "First Peace Corps/Dominican Republic." *Peace Corps Times:* WA DC, Jan.-Feb., 1985, p 5.

_____. "Remarks of President Ronald Reagan at Peace Corps Africa Send-off," *Peace Corps Times* WA DC, May-Jun., 1985, p 3.

_____. "25th Anniversary Begins in October." *Peace Corps Times:* WA DC, Jul.-Aug., 1985, p 5.

_____. "Water: The Essential Element, Peace Corps' Response." *Peace Corps Times:* WA DC, May-Jun., 1986, p 16-17.

_____. "Tuvalu RPCVs and Stamp Collectors." *Peace Corps Times:* WA DC, Jul.- Aug., 1986, p 9.

_____. "Networking: The Peace Corps Library." *Peace Corps Times:* WA DC, Jul.-Aug., 1989, p 19.

_____. "Save Your Journals." *Peace Corps Times:* WA DC, Nov.-Dec., 1989, p 3.

_____. "Humor in The Peace Corps." *Peace Corps Times:* WA DC, Jan.-Feb., 1990, p 3.

_____. "Rose Garden Sendoff For Poland and Hungary: Democratization Opens Doors To Central Europe." *Peace Corps Times:* WA DC, summer, 1989, p 18.

_____. "Peace Corps pushing environmental education efforts worldwide." *Peace Corps Times:* WA DC, Summer, 1990, p 24.

_____. "Desert Storm: Persian Gulf conflict causes temporary suspension of five Peace Corps Programs." *Peace Corps Times:* WA DC, spring, 1991, p 9-10.

_____. "Lotus Development Corporation Donates Software." *Peace Corps Times:* WA DC, Fall, 1992, p 5.

_____. "The World Map Project." *Peace Corps Times:* WA DC, May-Jun., 1989, p 16-17.

_____. "Networking: Peace Corps Volunteers and the Internet." *Peace Corps Times:* WA DC, fall, 1993, p 30.

_____. "Volunteers Featured in New Peace Corps Film." *Peace Corps Times:* WA DC, winter, 1994, p 39.

_____. "A Closer Look at What Peace Corps Volunteers Are Made of." *Peace Corps Times:* WA DC, winter, 1995, p 23.

_____. "Peace Corps Makes History in South Africa." *Peace Corps Times:* WA DC, spring, 1997, p 6.

_____. "Peace Corps Puts Its Stamp on the 60's." *Peace Corps Times:* WA DC, fall, 1999, p 1.

_____. "Crisis Corps Volunteers Lend Experience to Communities in Times of Need." *Peace Corps Times:* WA DC, Winter, 1998-1999, p 7.

_____. "Volunteers Celebrate Peace Corps Day." *Peace Corps Times:* WA DC, Summer, 2000, p 8.

_____. "Life Skills Manual: Education with a Message." *Peace Corps Times:* WA DC, Winter, 2005, p 1.

_____. "IT Specialists: The Challenges of Keeping Connected." *Peace Corps Times:* WA DC, Summer-Fall, 2006, p 2.

_____. "Peace Corps Policy on Technology Usage for Volunteers." *Peace Corps Times:* WA DC, Summer-Fall, 2006, p 3.

_____. "For PCVs, Every day is World AIDS Day." *Peace Corps Times:* WA DC, fall, 2007, p 3.

_____. "Agency News: Volunteer Numbers Reach 37-Year High." *Peace Corps Times* WA DC, fall, 2007, p 2.

_____. "World Map Project Spans Five Continents." *Peace Corps Times:* WA DC, Issue 1, 2010, p 1.

_____. "Applicant Numbers Grow." *Peace Corps Times:* WA DC, Issue 1, 2010, p 5.

_____. "Fellows/USA Celebrates 45 Years." *Peace Corps Times:* WA DC, Issue 2, 2010, p 5.

Awbrey, Stuart. "Politics and the Peace Corps." *Peace Corps Volunteer:* WA DC, Vol. V, No. 11, Sept., 1967, p 3.

Awbrey, Stuart & Brown, Pat. "The issues of Nigeria and beyond." *Peace Corps Volunteer:* WA DC, Vol. V, No. 2, Dec. 1966, p 2.

Barry, Daniel. "Brainwashing the Peace Corps." *The Nation*: May 7, 1983, p 572-573.

Benjamin, Judy. "A Peace Corps Forum Looks at 'The Internet as a Tool for Development'." *Peace Corps Times:* WA DC, Spring, 1995, p 28.

Cunningham, Patricia. "Radio Active: Peace Corps Volunteers Take to the Airwaves." *Peace Corps Times* WA DC, winter, 1996, p 16-19.

Flanigan, James C. "Jubilee! Peace Corps celebrates its 30th anniversary. Birthday event marked with cake, presidential proclamation." *Peace Corps Times:* WA DC, spring, 1991, p 4.

Grant, Walter. "Re-Entry Crisis." *The Peace Corps News:* Public Information Division, WA DC, Autumn, 1965, p 3.

Green, Romania, Hager, Michael, Hager, Vickie, Hancock, Michael, Olden, Dan. "The draft." *Peace Corps Volunteer:* WA DC, Vol. VI, No. 1, Nov., 1967, p 21.

Hert, Robert. "No room for Peace Corps." *Peace Corps Volunteer* WA DC, Vol. VII, No. 10, Sept., 1969, p 5.

Hewson, F. "Senior Citizens The Peace Corps Wants You!" *McCalls:* 107:60-1, Aug., 1980.

Jaffe, A. "Who Wants the Peace Corps?" *Newsweek:* NY, 15:42, Jun. 29, 1970.

Johns, Melissa. "Path to Empowerment." *Peace Corps Times:* WA DC, winter, 1996, p 12-14.

Keeton, Jon. "Seeds of Friendship." *Peace Corps Times:* WA DC, summer, 1992, p 8.

Londidier, Fred. "Complaints of draft." *Peace Corps Volunteer:* WA DC, Vol. V, No. 2, Dec., 1966, p 22.

McClure, Donovan. "Ankara, Turkey." *Peace Corps Volunteer:* WA DC, Vol. VII, No. 3, Jan., 1968, p 3-4.

McPherson, M. Peter. "Life As A PCV In Peru." *Peace Corps Times:* WA DC, Dec., 1985, p 15.

Prindle, Steve. "Cures for what ails us." *Peace Corps Volunteer:* WA DC, Vol. VII, No. 12, p 2.

Shakow, Alexander. "Training: almost the real thing." *Peace Corps Volunteer:* WA DC, Vol. VI, No. 6, Apr., 1968, p 4.

Tebbe, Susan & Flanigan, James C. "Exit from Zaire." *Peace Corps Times:* WA DC, Fall, 1991, p 13.

Tolley, Howard, Jr. "Letters to the volunteer: Political issue." *Peace Corps Volunteer:* WA DC, Vol. VII, No. 3, Jan., 1968, p 20.

Tolley, Howard, Jr. "Five Years of the Nixon Peace Corps." *Intellect:* 103:96-98, Nov. 8, 1974.

Weathers, O. & Borger, G. "The Peace Corps Grows Up." *Newsweek:* NY, 95:46, Jan. 7, 1980.

government reports

U.S. Congress. House. Subcommittee on Foreign Operations, Committee on Appropriations. *1st Annual Peace Corps Report.* 87th Congress, 2nd sess. U.S. Govt. Printing Office, WA DC, Jun. 30, 1962.

U.S. Congress. House. Subcommittee on Foreign Operations, Committee on Appropriations. *Peace Corps Fiscal Year 1966 Congressional Presentation.* 89th Congress, 1st Sess., U.S. Govt. Printing Office, WA DC, Apr., 1965.

U.S. Congress. House. Subcommittee on Foreign Operations, Committee on Appropriations. *Peace Corps Fiscal Year 1967 Congressional Presentation.* 89th Congress, 2nd Sess., U.S. Govt. Printing Office, WA DC, May, 1966.

U.S. Congress. House. Subcommittee on Foreign Operations, Committee on Appropriations. *Peace Corps Fiscal Year 1969 Congressional Presentation.* 90th Congress, 2nd Sess., U.S. Govt. Printing Office, WA DC, Mar., 1968.

U.S. Congress. House. Subcommittee on Foreign Operations, Committee on Appropriations. *Peace Corps Fiscal Year 1970 Congressional Presentation.* 91st Congress, 1st Sess., U.S. Govt. Printing Office, WA DC, May, 1969.

U.S. Congress. House. Subcommittee on Foreign Operations, Committee on Appropriations. *Peace Corps Fiscal Year 1971 Congressional Presentation.* 91st Congress, 2nd Sess., U.S. Govt. Printing Office, WA DC, Feb., 1970.

U.S. Congress. House. Subcommittee on Foreign Operations, Committee on Appropriations. *Action Fiscal Year 1974 Budget Peace Corps.* 93rd Congress, 1st Sess., U.S. Govt. Printing Office, WA DC, Mar., 1973.

U.S. Congress. House. Subcommittee on Foreign Operations, Committee on Appropriations. *Peace Corps Operations Report Fiscal Year 1973.* 93rd Congress, 1st Sess., U.S. Govt. Printing Office, WA DC, Jun., 1973.

U.S. Congress. House. Subcommittee on Foreign Operations, Committee on Appropriations. *Peace Corps Operations Report Fiscal Year 1975.* 93rd Congress, 2nd Sess., U.S. Govt. Printing Office, WA DC, Feb., 1974.

U.S. Congress. House. Subcommittee on Foreign Operations, Committee on Appropriations. *ACTION Fiscal Year 1976 Budget and Transition Estimate International Programs (Peace Corps) Submission to Congress.* 94th Congress, 1st Sess., U.S. Govt. Printing Office, WA DC, Feb. & Apr., 1975.

U.S. Congress. House. Subcommittee on Foreign Operations, Committee on Appropriations. *ACTION 1977 Annual Report.* 95th Congress, 1st Sess., U.S. Govt. Printing Office, WA DC, Jul., 1977.

U.S. Congress. House. Subcommittee on Foreign Operations. Committee on Appropriations. *ACTION Fiscal Year 1979 Budget Estimate International Programs (Peace Corps) Submission to Congress.* 96th Congress, 1st Sess., U.S. Govt. Printing Office, WA DC, Jan, 1979.

U.S. Congress. House. Subcommittee on Foreign Operations. Committee on Appropriations. *Peace Corps Fiscal Year 1981 Budget Estimate Submission to Congress.* 96th Congress, 2nd Sess., U.S. Govt. Printing Office, WA DC, Jan. 28, 1980.

U.S. Congress. House. Subcommittee on Foreign Operations, Committee on Appropriations. *Peace Corps Submission Budget Justification Fiscal Year 1982.* 97th Congress, 1st Sess., U.S. Govt. Printing Office, WA DC, Mar. 6, 1981.

U.S. Congress. House. Subcommittee on Foreign Operations. Committee on Appropriations. *Peace Corps Congressional Presentation Fiscal Year 1985.* 98th Congress, 2nd Sess., U.S. Govt. Printing Office, WA DC, Feb. 1, 1984.

U.S. Congress. House. Subcommittee on Foreign Operations. Committee on Appropriations. *Peace Corps Congressional Presentation Fiscal Year 1986.* 99th Congress, 2nd Sess., U.S. Govt. Printing Office, WA DC, Feb. 1, 1986.

U.S. Congress. House Subcommittee on Foreign Operations. Committee on Appropriations. *Peace Corps Congressional Presentation Fiscal Year 1990.* 101st Congress, 1st Sess., U.S. Govt. Printing Office, WA DC, Jan. 31, 1989.

U.S. Congress. House. Subcommittee on Foreign Operations. Committee on Appropriations. *Peace Corps Congressional Budget Presentation Fiscal*

Year 1997. 104th Congress, 2nd Sess., U.S. Govt. Printing Office, WA DC, Apr. 5, 1996.

U.S. Congress. House. Subcommittee on Foreign Operations. Committee on Appropriations. *Peace Corps Congressional Budget Presentation Fiscal Year 1999.* 105th Congress, 2nd Sess., U.S. Govt. Printing Office, WA DC, Feb. 6, 1998.

U.S. Congress. *Peace Corps Congressional Budget Justification Fiscal Year 2008.* 110th Congress, 2nd Sess., U.S. Govt. Printing Office, WA DC, no date.

U.S. Congress. House. Cynthia A. McKinney & Martin T. Meehan. *Report to Congressional Requests, Peace Corps Initiatives for Addressing Safety and Security Challenges Hold Promise but Progress Should be Assessed.* 107th Congress, 2nd Sess., G.A.O., Govt. Printing Office, WA DC, July, 2002.

U.S. Congress. House. Subcommittee on Foreign Operations. *The Peace Corps Performance and Accountability Report, Fiscal Year 2009.* 111th Congress, 1st Sess., U.S. Govt. Printing Office, WA DC, Nov. 16, 2009.

U.S. Congress. House. Subcommittee on Foreign Operations. *Final Audit: Peace Corps Volunteer Safety and Security Program, 1G-10-08-A.* 111th Congress, 2nd Sess., U.S. Govt. Printing Office, Washington D.C., April, 2010.

U.S. Congress. House. Subcommittee on Foreign Operations. Committee on Appropriations. *The Peace Corps: A Comprehensive Agency Assessment Final Report.* 111th Congress, 2nd Sess., U.S. Govt. Printing Office, WA, DC, June, 2010.

U.S. Peace Corps. *The Safety of the Volunteer 2007 Annual Report of Volunteer Safety.* Peace Corps Office of Safety and Security, Crime Statistics and Analysis Unit, U.S. Govt. Printing Office, WA DC, 2007.

journals

Calvert, Laura D. "Notes on the Peace Corps Language Training Program." *The Modern Language Journal*, Vol. 47, No. 7, (Nov., 1963), p 319-323.

Harris, Jesse G. "A Science of the South Pacific: Analysis of the Character Structure of the Peace Corps Volunteer." *American Psychologist*, 1973 Mar 28(3).

Smith, Sandy. "The Peace Corps: Benign Development?" *The Multinational Monitor*, Vol. &, No. 13, Sept., 1986, 11 pages.

electronic

_____. "Overview." *Peace Corps Journals.* No post date, 1 p, Internet 05-26-2010, http://www.peacecorpsjournals.com/?about .

_____."Honoring Their Service: Fallen Peace Corps Volunteers." *Peace Corps Connect.* No post date, 5 p, Internet 05-23-2010, http://www.peacecorpsconnect.org/node/5306 .

_____. "Gaddi Vasquez." *Wikipedia.* No post date, 1 p. Internet 05-28-2010, http://www.en.wikipedia.org/wiki/Gaddi_Vasquez .

_____."Peace Corps 40th has been postponed." *PCOL Magazine*. Posted 09-14-2001, 1 p, Internet 05-26-2010. http://www.peacecorpsonline.org/messages/2629/5453.html?1000332542.

_____."Robert Sargent Shriver Jr calls for a new Peace Corps." *PCOL Magazine*. Posted 11-15-2001, 11 p, Internet 05-26-2010, http://www.peacecorpsonline.org/messages/2629/6147.html .

_____. "Half Page Ad of RPCVs opposing War in Iraq runs in NY Times." *PCOL Magazine*. Posted 02-21-2003, 16 p, Internet 05-28-2010, http://www.peacecorpsonline.org/messags/messages/2629/1012034.html .

_____. "India RPCV Stephen Downs arrested in mall for wearing anti-war t-shirt." *PCOL Magazine*. Posted 03-05-2003, 6 p, Internet 05-28-2010, http://www.peacecorpsonline.org/messages/messages/2629/2012353.html .

_____. "Second Ad of RPCVs opposing War in Iraq runs in NY Times." *PCOL Magazine*. Posted 03-14-2003, 8 p, Internet 05-28-2010, http://www.peacecorpsonline.org/messages/messages/2629/2012516.html .

_____. "The Nation: Pre-empting Protest at the Peace Corps." *PCOL Magazine*. Posted 05-19-2003, 8 p, Internet 05-28-2010, http://www.peacecorpsonline.org/messages/messages/2629/2013629.html .

_____. "Philippines RPCV Ryan Clancy fined $10,000 for protesting war in Iraq." *PCOL Magazine*. Posted 08-12-2003, 7 p, Internet 05-28-2010, http://www.peacecorpsonline.org/messages/messages/2629/2015375.html .

_____. "A Chronology of the Peace Corps 1961-2003," *Dayton Daily News*, posted 10-24-2003, 2 p, Internet 04-30-2010, http://www.dayton .

_____. US Congress Scrutinizes Peace Corps Volunteers' Security." *Newsom*. Posted 03-24-2004, 3 p, Internet 05-28-2010, http://www1.voanews.com/english/news/a-13-a-2004-03-24-3-US-67492777.html?moddat .

_____. "971 Peace Corps Volunteer writers by country." *Peace Corps Writers*. Posted 2008, various pages, Internet 06-15-2010, http://www.peacecorpswriters.org/pages/depts/resources/country.html .

_____. "Peace Corps To End HIV Discrimination." *365gay Newscenter*. Posted 07-31-2008, 7 p, Internet 05-28-2010, http://www.peacecorpsonline.org/messages/messages/467/3210416.html.

_____. "Where do Peace Corps Volunteers go?" *U.S. Peace Corps*. Posted 09-14-2008, Internet 05-20-2010, http://www.peacecorps.gov .

_____. "1970's." *U.S. Peace Corps*. Posted 09-27-2008, 1 p, Internet 05-07-2010, http://www.peacecorps.gov/index.cfm?shell=learn.whatispc.history.decades.1970 .

_____. "Past Directors." *U.S. Peace Corps*. Posted 10-22-2009, 4 p, Internet 04-30-2010, http://www.peacecorps.gov/index.cfm?shell=learn.whatispchistory.Pastdir .

_____. "Film festival to showcase Peace Corps volunteer's stories." *Columbia Missourian*. Posted 11-12-2009, 7 p, Internet 06-01-2010, http://www.columbiamissourian.com/stories/2009/22/12/bringing it home/ .

_____. "Fallen Peace Corps Volunteers Memorial Project." *Fallen Peace Corps Volunteers Memorial Project Inc.* Posted 11-22-2009, 4 p, Internet 05-04-2010, http://www.fpcv.org/ .

_____. "Peace Corps Is Supportive of Change." *First Response Action.* Posted 04-15-2010, 7 p, Internet 05-28-2010, http://firstresponseaction.blogspot. com/2010/04/peace-corps-is-supportive-of-change.html .

_____."Peace Corps." *Wikipedia.* Posted 04-29-2010, 17 p, Internet 04-30-2010, http://en.wikipedia.org/wiki/Peace_Corps .

Anderson, Jeffery. "Safety at risk for Peace Corps volunteers." *Washington Times.* Posted 06-17-2010, Internet 06-18-2010, 2 p, http://www.washingtontimes. com/news/2010/jun17/volunteers-for-peace-corps-at-risk-ofviolence...

Anderson, Michele. "Citizens Opposed to War with Iraq walk for peace, plan Forum." *Keweenaw NOW,* Posted 10-12-2002, 6 p, Internet 05-28-2010, http:// www.keweenaw.com/news/peace_walk_10_12_02/peace_walk_10_12_02. htm .

Anderson, Ron. "Don't Think/Some Days: A Late 60's Film Portrait of Peace Corps Lifestyle." No post date, 1 p, Internet 06-01-2010, http://www. ronandersonservices.com/pc_film .

Carollo, Russell & Hopgood, Mel-Ling. "Mission of sacrifice." *Dayton Daily News:* Oct. 26, 2003,Dayton,OH, no post date, 15 p, Internet 05-28-2010 http://www.daytondailynews.com/project/content/project/peacecorps/ daily/1026main.html.

Coyne, John. "The infamous Peace Corps postcard." *Peace Corps Writers.* No post date, 2 p, Internet 06-20-2010, http://www.peacecorpswriters.org .

Democracy Now! The War and Peace Report. "US Embassy in Bolivia Tells Fulbright Scholar and Peace Corps Volunteers to Spy on Venezuelans and Cubans in Bolivia." *Public Broadcasting System.* Posted 02-11-2008, 1 p, Internet 05-28-2010, http://www.democracynow.org/2008/2/11/us_embassy_ in_bolivis_tells_Fulbright .

Gerring, Joan P., Dr. "Improvements Needed in Peace Corps Support Services." *PCOL Magazine.* Posted 12-01-2002, 28 p, Internet 06-20-2010, http:// peacecorpsonline.org/messages/messages/2629/1010839.html .

Hargarten, S.W. & Baker, S.P.. "Fatalities in the peace corps. A retrospective study: 1962 through 1983." *The Journal of the American Medical Association.* Abstract. 1985 Sep. 13;254(10):1326-0. No post date, National Library of Medicine, National Institute of Health, 1 p, Internet 06-18-2010, http://www. ncbi.nlm.gov/pubmed/4021010 .

Koerten, Jared. "Anti-Communism and Idealism: The Peace Corps and U.S. Foreign Policy in the Third World, 1960-1966." University of Wisconsin, May, 2009. No post date, 30 p, Internet 07-07-2010, http://www.icpsr.umich. edu/files/ICPSR/prize/koerten_paper.pdf .

Ludam, Chuck. "Peace Corps Early Termination Rates: Country by Country." *Peace Corps Wikipedia.* Posted 12-10-2009, Final Department of State Foreign Operations and Related Programs Appropriations Act, 2010, 1 p, Internet 04-30-2010, http://www.peacecorpswiki.com/Congressional_Appropriations .

Nurthen, N.M. & Jung, P. "Fatalities in the Peace Corps: a retrospective study, 1984 to 2003." *The Journal of Travel Medicine.* Abstract. 2008 Mar-Apr,15(2):95-101. U.S. National Library of Medicine, National Institute of

Health, No post date, 1p, Internet 06-18-2010, http://www.ncbi.nlm.nih.gov/ pubmed/18346242 .

Sheppard, Michael. "Early Termination in the Peace Corps," Department of Statistics and Probability," No posting date. *Michigan State University*, May, 2008, 16 p, Internet 04-30-2010, http://www.sribd.com/doc/22535669/Peace-Corps-Early-Termination-Computations-et.

Tarnoff, Curt, "CRS Report for Congress-The Peace Corps: Current Issues," RS21168, Congressional Research Service for the Library of Congress, Updated 11-14- 2008, 6 p, Internet 06-10-2010, http://www.fas.org/sgp/crs/ RS21168.pdf .

Waldorf, Saral. "My time in the Peace Corps." *CBS Money Watch*. Posted winter, 2001, 7 p, Internet 06-20-2010, http://findarticles.com/p/articles/mi_m0377/ is_2001_Wntr/ai_69411631

Welti, Adam J. "Reevaluating the Peace Corps." *Campus Progress*. Posted 10-09-2008, 8 p, Internet 06-20-2010, http://www.campusprogress.org/ fiedlreport/3273/reevaluating-the-peace-corps... .

interviews

Coyne, John P. (former PC volunteer & staff, Editor *RPCV Writers* and *Peace Corps Worldwide)*, telephone, May 17, 2010.

Haley Beil, Marian. (former PC volunteer & staff, Publisher *RPCV Writers* and *Peace Corps Worldwide*), electronic, May 17, 2010.

Meisler, Stanley. (former PC staff, author), telephone, May 12, 2010.

Pickens, Hugh. (former PC volunteer, Editor/Publisher *PCOL Magazine*), electronic, May 19 & 28, 2010.

Quigley, Kevin. (former PC volunteer, President National Peace Corps Association), electronic, May 18, 2010.

Searles, P. David. (former PC staff, author), electronic, May 13, 16, 30, 31, 2010.

PEACE CORPS GOALS

Peace Corps Goals

1. Helping the people of interested countries in meeting their need for trained men and women.
2. Helping promote a better understanding of Americans on the part of the people served.
3. Helping promote a better understanding of other peoples on the part of Americans.

   SOURCE: Peace Corps Electronic Archives (Peace Corps.gov/mission)

MAPS, LISTS & GRAPHS

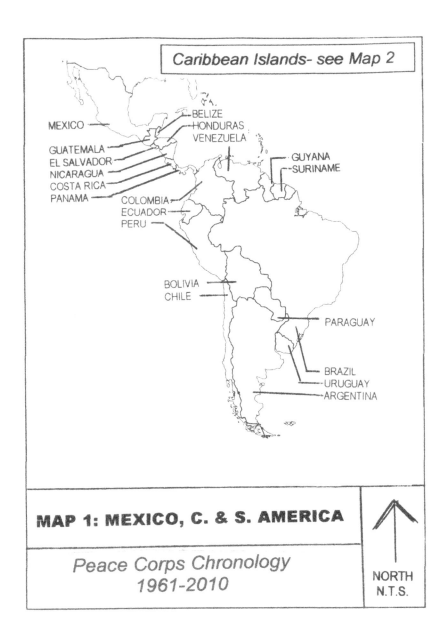

Caribbean Islands- see Map 2

MEXICO
BELIZE
HONDURAS
VENEZUELA
GUATEMALA
EL SALVADOR
NICARAGUA
COSTA RICA
PANAMA
GUYANA
SURINAME
COLOMBIA
ECUADOR
PERU
BOLIVIA
CHILE
PARAGUAY
BRAZIL
URUGUAY
ARGENTINA

MAP 1: MEXICO, C. & S. AMERICA

Peace Corps Chronology
1961-2010

NORTH
N.T.S.

77

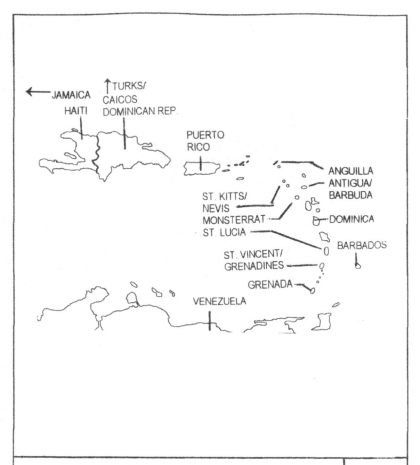

MAP 2: CARIBBEAN ISLANDS

Peace Corps Chronology
1961-2010

NORTH
N.T.S.

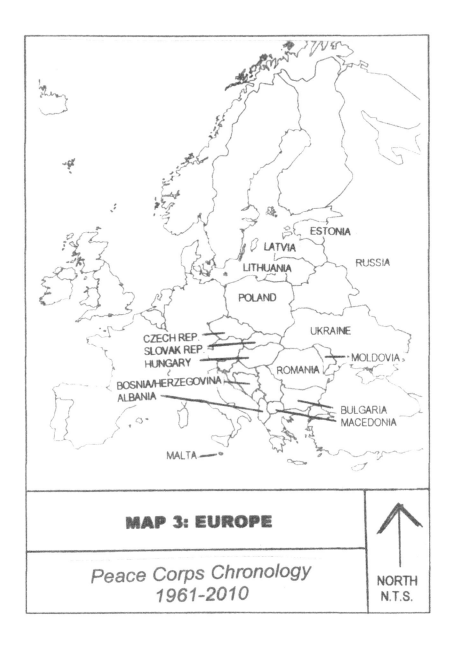

MAP 3: EUROPE

Peace Corps Chronology
1961-2010

NORTH
N.T.S.

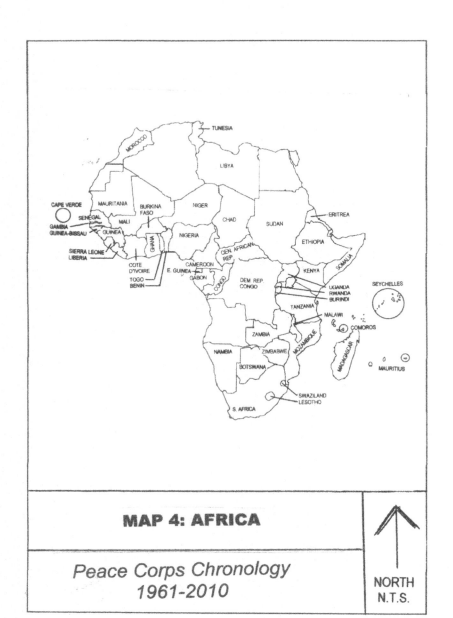

MAP 4: AFRICA

Peace Corps Chronology
1961-2010

NORTH
N.T.S.

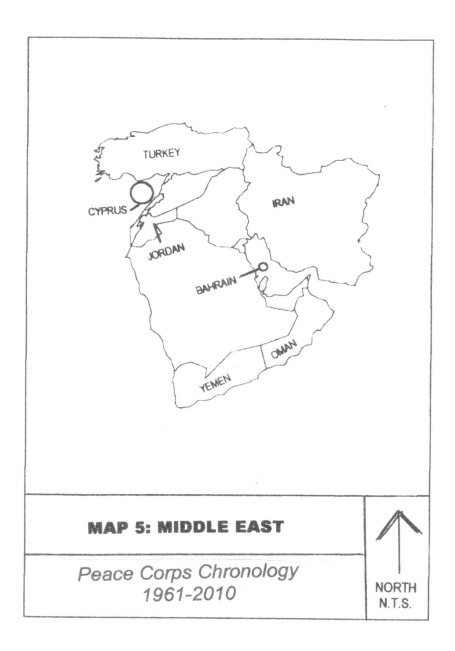

MAP 5: MIDDLE EAST

*Peace Corps Chronology
1961-2010*

NORTH
N.T.S.

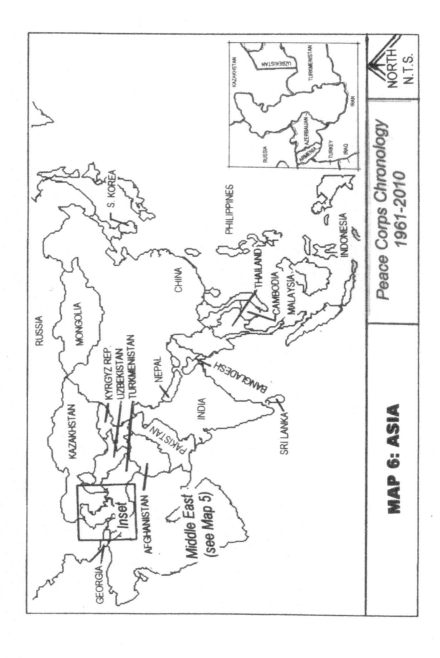

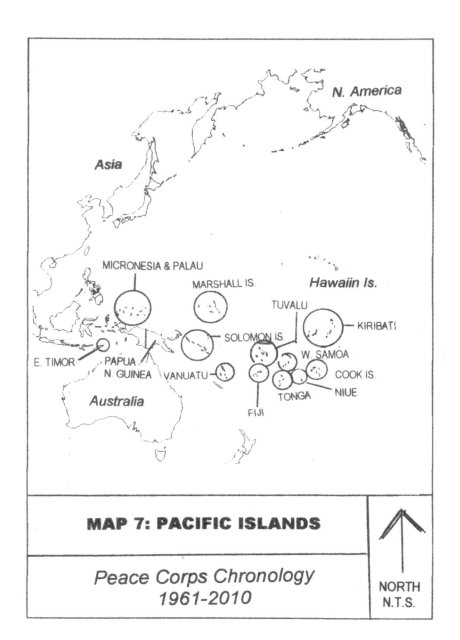

Where & when they served
(# of volunteers 1961- 2008)

COUNTRY	FORMER NAME (1960)	SERVICE DATES	TOT. # VOL.
CARIBBEAN			
Anguilla		1967-present	n/a
Antigua/Barbuda		1967-present	n/a
Barbados		1965-present	n/a
Dominica		1967-present	n/a
Dominican Rep.		1962-present	4,042
Grenada		1963-1982	n/a
		1984-present	n/a
Haiti		1983-1987	507
Jamaica		1962-present	3,635
Montserrat		1967-present	n/a
St. Christopher/		1967-present	n/a
Nevis			
St. Lucia		1961-present	n/a
St. Vincent/		1967-present	n/a
The Grenadines			
Turks& Caicos		1980-present	n/a
SUBTOTAL E. CARIBBEAN			3,638
TOTAL			11,822
MEXICO & CENTRAL AMERICA			
Belize	Br. Honduras	1962-present	2,066
Costa Rica		1963-present	3,254
El Salvador		1962-1980	
		1993-present	2,066
Guatemala		1963-present	4,561
Honduras		1963-present	5,571
Mexico		2004-present	119
Nicaragua		1968-1979	
		1991-present	1,909

Panama		1963-1971	1,818
TOTAL			21,364

SOUTH AMERICA

Argentina		1992-1994	38
Bolivia		1962-1971	
		1990-2008	2,702
Brazil		1962-1981	4,150
Chile		1961-1982	
		1991-1998	2,096
Colombia		1961-1981	
		2010	4,638
Ecuador		1962-present	5,789
Guyana	Br. Guiana	1967-1971	
		1995-present	538
Paraguay		1967-present	3,357
Peru		1962-1975	
		2002-present	2,810
Suriname	Dut. Guiana	1995-present	361
Uruguay		1963-1974	
		1991-1997	338
Venezuela		1962-1977	2,134
TOTAL			28,951

AFRICA

Benin	Dahomey	1968-present	1,687
Botswana	Bechuanaland	1966-1997	
		2003-present	2,097
Burkina Faso	Upper Volta	1967-1987	
		1995-present	1,584
Burundi	Ruanda Urundi	1983-1993	150
Cameroon		1962-present	3,091
Cape Verde		1988-present	475
Cen. African Rep.		1972-1996	906
Chad		1966-1979	
		1987-1990	
		1990-1996	
		2003-2006	726

85

Comoros		1988-1995	79
Cote d'Ivoire	Ivory Coast	1962-1981	
		1990-2003	1,533
Dem. Rep. of Congo	Congo/Zaire	1970-1991	2,530
Equitorial Guinea	Sp. Guinea	1988-1993	61
Eritrea	Ethiopia	1995-1998	86
Ethiopia		1962-1977	
		1995-1999	
		2007-present	3,012
Gabon		1963-1967	
		1973-2005	1,460
The Gambia	Gambia	1967-present	1,480
Ghana		1961-present	4,056
Guinea		1963-1966	
		1969-1971	
		1985-2009	1,287
Guinea Bissau	Port-Guinea	1988-1998	177
Kenya		1964-present	4,877
Lesotho	Basutoland	1967-present	2,112
Liberia		1962-1990	
		2008-present	3,832
Libya		1966-1969	295
Madagascar		1993-2009	
		2009-present	815
Malawi	Nyasaland	1963-1972	
		1973-1976	
		1978-present	2,388
Mali	Mali Federation	1971-present	2,379
Mauritania		1967-1967	
		1971-1991	
		1991-2009	1,259
Mauritius		1971-1975	48
Morocco		1963-present	4,177
Mozambique		1998-present	558
Namibia	S-W Africa	1990-present	1,150
Niger		1962-present	3,058
Nigeria		1961-1971	
		1992-1995	2,094

Rep. of Congo	Congo	1991-1997	139
Rwanda	Ruanda Urundi	1975-1993	
		2008-present	149
Senegal	Mali Federation	1963-present	2,969
Seychelles		1974-1996	49
Sierra Leone		1962-1992	
		1992-1994	
		2010	3,479
Somali Rep.		1962-1970	357
S. Africa	Union S. Africa	1997-present	847
Sudan		1984-1986	8
Swaziland		1969-1996	
		2003-present	1,404
Tanzania	Tanganyika	1961-1970	
		1979-present	2,202
Togo		1962-present	2,580
Tunisia		1962-1991	
		1991-1996	2,130
Uganda		1964-1973	
		1991-1999	
		2000-present	1,004
Zambia	Fed. Rhodesia	1993-present	1,028
Zimbabwe	Fed. Rhodesia	1991-2002	366
TOTAL			74,230

EUROPE

Albania		1992-1997	
		2003-present	391
Bosnia-Herzegovina	Yugoslavia	2000-2002	21
Bulgaria		1991-present	1,156
Czech Rep.	Czechoslovakia	1990-1997	234
Estonia	Soviet Union	1992-2002	175
Hungary		1990-1997	354
Latvia	Soviet Union	1992-2002	217
Lithuania	Soviet Union	1992-2002	219
Macedonia	Yugoslavia	1996-present	390
Malta		1972-1974	
		1989-1998	26

Moldova	Soviet Union	1993-present	963
Poland		1990-2001	963
Romania		1991-present	1,087
Russia		1992-2003	729
Slovak Rep.	Czechoslovakia	1990-2002	329
Ukraine	Soviet Union	1992-present	2,045
TOTAL			9,299

MIDDLE EAST

Bahrain		1974-1979	68
Cyprus		1962-1964	29
Iran		1962-1976	1,748
Jordan		1997-2002	
		2004-present	419
Oman		1973-1983	160
Turkey		1962-1972	1,460
Yemen		1973-1994	564
TOTAL			4,448

ASIA

Afghanistan		1962-1979	1.652
Armenia	Soviet Union	1992-present	679
Azerbaijan	Soviet Union	2003-present	316
Bangladesh	E. Pakistan	1996-2006	280
Cambodia		2006-present	81
China		1993-present	586
Georgia	Soviet Union	2001-present	337
India		1961-1976	4,325
Indonesia		1963-1965	
		2010-	36
Kazakhstan	Soviet Union	1993-present	1,043
Kyrgyz Rep.	Soviet Union	1993-present	831
Malaysia	Fed. of Malaya	1962-1983	4,067
Mongolia		1991-present	794
Nepal		1962-2005	3,629
Pakistan		1961-1967	
		1988-1991	517
Philippines		1961-1990	

		1992-present	8,369
S. Korea		1966-1981	2,068
Sri Lanka	Ceylon	1962-1964	
		1967-1970	
		1983-1998	372
Thailand		1962-present	4,915
Turkmenistan	Soviet Union	1993-present	698
Uzbekistan	Soviet Union	1992-2005	767
TOTAL			36,362

PACIFIC ISLANDS

Cook Is.		1982-1986	
		1988-1995	33
E. Timor	Port. Timor	2002-2006	104
Fiji		1968-1998	2,231
Kiribati	Gilbert Is.	1967-2008	489
Marshall Is.		1966-1996	149
Micronesia &			
Palau	Caroline Is.	1966-present	4,203
Niue		1994-2002	19
Papua N.Guinea		1981-2001	701
W.Samoa	Samoa	1967-present	1,717
Solomon Is.		1971-2000	744
Tonga		1967-present	1,536
Tuvalu	Ellice Is.	1974-1997	43
Vanuatu	New Hebrides	1990-present	533
TOTAL			12,502

WORLD-WIDE TOTAL 1961-2008   198,978

SOURCE: Peace Corps Electronic Archives (Peace Corps.gov)

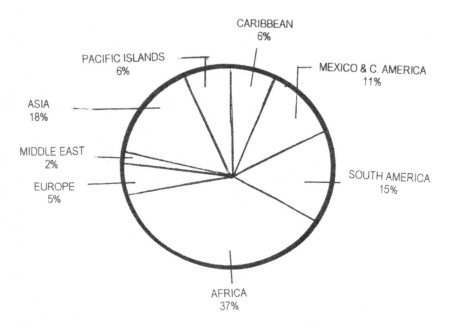

Figure 1: % of volunteers by region
(1961-2008)

MOST VOLUNTEERS PER COUNTRY
1961-2008

1.	PHILIPPINES	8,369
2.	ECUADOR	5,789
3.	HONDURAS	5,571
4.	THAILAND	4,915
5.	KENYA	4,877
6.	COLOMBIA	4,638
7.	GUATEMALA	4,561
8.	INDIA	4,325
9.	PALAU	4,203
10.	MOROCCO	4,177

SOURCE: Peace Corps Electronic Archives (Peace Corps.gov)

Number of volunteers per year

1962	2,940		1997	6,660*
1963	6,646		1998	6,719*
1964	10,078		1999	6,989*
1965	13,248		2000	7,164*
1966	15,556		2001	6,643*
1967	14,968		2002	6,636*
1968	13,823		2003	7,533*
1969	12,131		2004	7,733*
1970	9,513		2005	7,810*
1971	7.066		2006	7,628*
1972	6,894		2007	7,896*
1973	7,341		2008	7,876*
1974	8,044		2009	7,671*
1975	7,015			
1976	5,958			
1977	5,752			
1978	7,072			
1979	6,328			
1980	5,994			
1981	5,445			
1982	5,380			
1983	5,483			
1984	5,699			
1985	6,264			
1986	5,913			
1987	5,219			
1988	5,812			
1989	6,248			
1990	5,583			
1991	5,866			
1992	5,831			
1993	6,467			
1994	6,745			
1995	7,218			
1996	6,910			

SOURCES:
Elizabeth Cobbs Hoffman,
*All You Need Is Love: The
Peace Corps and the Spirit
of the 1960s*
Stanley Meisler.

Figure 2: Average # of volunteers/decade

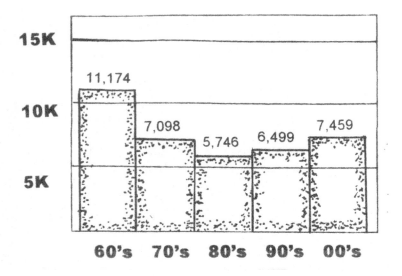

Figure 3: # of volunteers/year

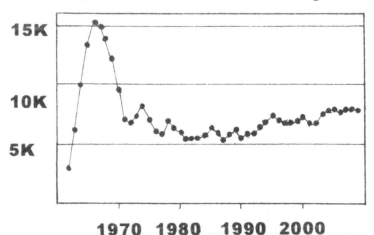

SOURCES: *All You Need Is Love; The Peace Corps and the Spirit of the 1960's*, Elizabeth Cobbs Hoffman & Stanley Meisler

Figure 4: Average volunteer age/ selected years

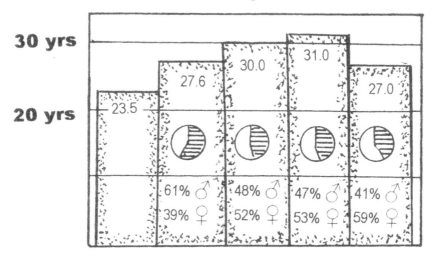

SOURCE: Peace Corps magazines

Lawrence F. Lihosit

Figure 5: % of volunteers per work sector/ selected years

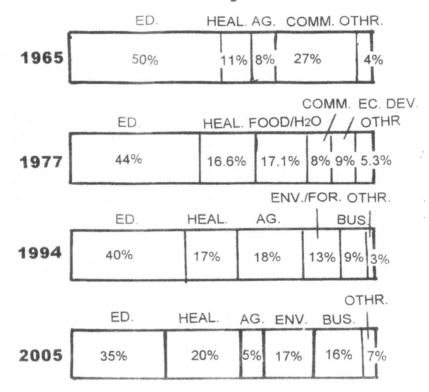

ED.= EDUCATION
HEAL.= HEALTH
FOOD/H20= FOOD & WATER
AG.= AGRICULTURE
COMM.= COMMUNITY ACTION OR SERVICE
EC. DEV.= ECONOMIC DEVELOPMENT
ENV./FOR.= ENVIRONMENT & FORESTRY
BUS.= BUSINESS
OTHR.- OTHER

SOURCE: Peace Corps Annual Reports & PC Times

ABOUT THE AUTHOR

The Author was born in the southern suburbs of Chicago, Illinois in 1951. His family later moved to Arizona where he graduated from grade school, high school and Arizona State University. He reluctantly served in the U.S. Army Reserves during the closing years of the Vietnam War and enthusiastically volunteered for the Peace Corps (Honduras, 1975-1977). His travels and work have taken him from the salmon spawning Nushagak River Basin in southwestern Alaska to the fertile Argentine Pampas. His continuing studies have included master's coursework in urban planning at *la Universidad Nacional Autónoma de México* in Mexico City, art and creative writing at Skyline College in San Bruno, California and education at California State University Fresno. He has earned his living as an urban planner for many years, working in Honduras, Mexico, Alaska, Arizona and California.

Also by the author

Americruise, (1993), travel memoir.

Salt of the Earth, (1994), oral history.

Travels in South America, (1995), travel narrative.

*American Papers, (1996-1998), essays.

Travelin' Doodles, (1997), sketches.

*Across the Yucatan, (2007), travel narrative.

*Attack of the Claw, (2008), poetry.

*Jesus was Arrested in Mexico City and Missed
the Wedding, (2008), travel narrative.

☺Whispering Campaign; Stories from Mesoamerica, (2009), fiction.

☺South of the Frontera; A Peace Corps Memoir, (2010), travel memoir.

☺Years On and Other Essays, (2011), travel essays.

*Available from A Book Company
1625 Howard Road, Suite 257
Madera, CA 93637

☺Published by iUniverse and available on Amazon.com

A Book Company: Literature for us folks.
*"If our society is rude, much wisdom is not necessary to supply our wants
and a fool can sometimes put on his clothes better than a wise man can do it
for him."* Newspaper Extracts III, Maryland Journal, December 19, 1783.
Printed in the United States of America

INDEX

A

Abell, Richard 32
Ackerman, William 15
ACTION 21, 28
Addams, James 1
Adkins, Darryl 32
Afghanistan 9, 18, 24, 29
Agnew, Spiro 18
Albania 41, 45, 51
Albertson, Maurice 2
Aldrich, Elizabeth 22
Ammon, Wyatt 52
Anguilla 14
Ann Arbor, Michigan 34
Antigua/Barbuda 14
Arab Republic 23
Argentina 41, 42
Armenia 41
Ashton, Thomas 13
Atlanta, Georgia 49
Azerbaijan 51

B

Baciewicz, Marian 30
Bahler, Bethanne 24
Bahrain 24, 29
Baker, Gregor V. 52
Baker, Gregory V. 23

Bangladesh 53
Banner, Alan C. 22
Barakatt, Thomas 42
Barbados 12
Barnum, Florice 13
Beckner, John 15
Belize 9, 27, 56
Bellamy, Carol 41, 43
Benin 15, 23, 25, 57
Benson, Robert 27
Bessmertnykh, Alexander 39
Bhansali, Justin 47
Birky, Pauline E. 2
Bissau 37, 45
Blake, Denise 24
Blatchford, Joseph 16, 17, 19, 20, 21,
    62
Blum, John 14
Bock, Robert 46
Bogenschneider, David 20
Bolivia 9, 12, 18, 20, 21, 39, 40, 51,
    54
Bond, Paul 12
Bosch, Judith 19
Botswana 12, 29, 33, 45, 51, 56
Bowers, Elizabeth 49
Bowles, Chester 2
Boyd, Nancy 10
Bradfield, George 25

Brady, Justin 53
Brazil 9, 27, 29, 31
Bruce, Jeffrey 51
Bryan, Jerry 27
Bulgaria 40
Burkina Faso 14, 25, 36, 43
Burundi 33, 41
Bush, George H. 38
Butler, Steven 37

C

Cambodia 18, 53
Cameroon 9, 12, 25, 35, 36, 43
Campbell, Julia 54
Cape Verde 37
Carmona, Margaret 31
Carpenter, Thomas 25
Cecchini, Ronald 34
Celeste, Richard F. 28, 30, 31
Central African Republic 22, 36, 44
Chad 12, 29, 36, 38, 39, 44, 51, 53
Chaljub, Paul 32
Challed, William 22
Chance, Stephanie 60
Chao, Elaine 40, 41
Chezem, Jacqueline 25
Chile 2, 8, 9, 12, 13, 25, 27, 32, 40, 45
China 32, 41, 42, 54
Chow, Joseph 57
Christie, Barbara 25
Church, Frank 17
Clinton, Hillary Rodham 43
Clutterbuck, Marie 19
Colombia 2, 8, 9, 10, 15, 18, 26, 27, 31, 60
Colorado State University Research Foundation 2, 5, 7, 54
Columbia University 34
Committee of Returned Volunteers 18, 19
Comoros 37, 43
Consolidated Appropriations Act 57
Consolidated Appropriations Bill 50, 51
Cook Islands 32, 36, 37, 43

Cooper, Cooper 54
Cooper, Theodore 31
Copeland, Audrey 35
Corbin, Jeanne 32
Corley, Judith 12
Costa, Mathew 53
Costa Rica 10, 23, 25, 45
Cote dâ€™Ivoire 9, 24, 25, 31, 39, 41, 46, 47, 51
Courtway, Rene 23
Coutu, Nancy 44
Coverdell, Paul D. 37, 40
Coyne, John P. 70
Crawford, Brenda 37
Craw, Nick 23, 24
Crimmins, Roseanne 14
Cronin, Thomas 25
Cross, June 25
Crotty, Kathryn 33
Crozier, David 9
Cyprus 9, 11
Cyr, Philip 32
Czech Republic 45

D

Darling, Joy 12
Davey, Susan 19
Davidson, John 22
Davis, Robert 25
Dellenback, John 24, 26
Democratic Republic of the Congo 19, 40
Detjen, Frederick 10
DiDiego, William 47
Dodd, Chris 31
Dominican Republic 9, 12, 14, 23, 24, 34, 36, 38, 45, 50
Drabiski, Michelle 38
Driscoll, James 12
Dunn, Lowell 13

E

Eastern Caribbean 29
East Timor 49, 53

E. Caribbean 13, 25, 27
Ecuador 9, 12, 22, 27, 30, 32, 35, 52
Edens, Brian 32
Edstrand, Mark 33
Edwards, David 40
El Salvador 9, 15, 18, 28, 29, 30, 41, 48
English, Joseph 11
Equitorial Guinea 37
Eritrea 43, 45
Escondido, California 20
Estonia 41
Ethiopia 9, 13, 14, 22, 23, 27, 43, 46, 54

F

Fagan, Susan 48
Fahey, Diane 25
Farrar, Henry 18
Fiji 15, 27, 30, 45
Fillmore, Diana 30
Fink, Linda 23
First Response Action 58, 69
Flynn, Gerald 12
Fort Collins, Colorado 5, 54, 55
Foss, Marilyn 54

G

Gabon 10, 14, 23, 30, 46, 52
Galgas, Eugene 27
Gamber, H. Benjamin 25
Gambia 14, 29, 31, 32
Gardner, Deborah 25
Gavit, Francis 25
Gearan, Mark D. 43, 46
Georgia 48
Gerring, Joan P. 44, 45
Ghana 8, 9, 14, 21, 27, 30, 48
Gliessman, Lester 27
Glotfelty, Scott 37
Goldwater, Barry 7
Gould, Bruce 14
Grenada 10, 32, 34

Grenadines 14
Gross, Gail 19
Guatemala 10, 25, 29, 32, 33, 34, 36, 42, 43
Guayana 20
Guinea 10, 12, 16, 17, 21, 31, 32, 35, 37, 41, 45, 47, 57
Guyana 14, 21, 43

H

Haggard, Marshall 32
Hahn, Kalman 21
Haiti 2, 33, 36
Hale, John S. 40
Haley Beil, Marian 70
Hamer, Stephen 25
Hancock, Michigan 49
Harding, Susan 41
Hassett, Thomas 13
Hellyer, William 15
Henrietta, James 21
Herzegovina 47, 49
Hess, Diana 33
Hess, Donald 22, 23
Higher Education Act 35
Hill, Helene 46
Hoffman, James 25
Holland, Philip 21
Honduras 10, 14, 17, 25, 27, 36, 37, 44
Horan, Tessa 53
House Foreign Affairs Committee 23
Hughes, James 12
Humphrey, Don 12
Humphrey, Hubert 1
Hungary 39, 43, 45
Hushaw, Harry 32
Hyatt, Janis 32

I

India 8, 9, 11, 14, 15, 18, 21, 24, 25
Indira Gandhi 15
Indonesia 10, 12, 60
Iran 9, 12, 13, 14, 19, 22, 25

J

Jacoby, Curtis 24
Jaffe, Larisa 48
Jamaica 9, 19, 24, 32, 36
James, William 1
Jandorf, Daniel 19
Johannesburg, South Africa. 44
Johnson, Lyndon Baines 15
Johnson, Mary 42
Johnson, Paul 25
Johnson, Wilburn 23
Jonas, Robert 27
Jordan 45, 49, 52

K

Kallison, Joie 46
Karrer, Andrew 37
Kazakhstan 41
Kelly, Richard 27
Kennedy, John F. 2, 7, 8
Kenney, Ann 21
Kenya 11, 12, 20, 22, 25, 27, 33, 39, 48
Kim, So-Youn 57
Kinsey, Peverly 13
Kiribati 14, 23, 56
Kirking, Francis 12
Kossowska, Danuta 37
Kotzian, Michael 18
Kowalczyk, Stanley 12
Krok, Florence 27
Krow, Brian 46
Kruger, Raymond 35
Kuhn, Ronald 21
Kyrgyz Republic 41, 55

L

Laffey, Thomas 15
Lane, Lois Ann 29
Larson, Curtis 12
Larson, David 14
Latvia 41, 49
Lawyer, Terry 22

Leahy, Richard 22
Lee, Barbara 59
Lee, Jang 48
Lesotho 14, 30, 33, 34, 45, 47
LeSuer, Thomas 30
Leveille, Kevin 46
Liberia 9, 19, 21, 25, 27, 33, 39, 56
Libya 12, 17
Liechtenstein 15
Lillig, Robert 22
Lindstrom, Robert 44
Lithuania 41, 49
Livingston, Elizabeth 45
Lockhart, Thomas 30
Long, Robert 33
Losikoff, Susan 18
Luecke, Christopher 27

M

MacGillivary, Kathryn 46
Mack, Jeremiah 45
Madagascar 41, 44
Maggard, Phillip 10
Malawi 10, 15, 17, 22, 23, 25, 27, 41, 46, 47
Malaysia 8, 9, 15, 18, 20, 25, 33
Mali 21, 32, 33, 51, 53
Mali, 21
Malone, Stephen 25
Malta 22, 24, 38, 45
Manke, Linda 22
Maresco, Thomas 60
Marshall Islands 12, 44
Marshall, John 32
Masover, Lynne 30
Mathis, William 34
Matthews, Timothy 29
Mauritania 13, 14, 20, 21, 39, 40, 57
Mauritius 20, 21, 22, 25, 40
McCarthy, David 19
McClellan, Bridgette 32
Mc Dearman, Ronald G. 48
McFate, Robert 27
McKay, Marilyn 19

McKeen, Bruce 11
McMahon, Brien 1
McManua, Roger 10
Meisler, Stanley 70
Merrill, Martha 19
Merrill, Zack 51
Messer, Steven 23
Mexico 2, 48, 52
Micronesia 12, 19, 22, 30, 33, 37
Miller, Zell 49
Millikan, Max 2
Moldova 41
Mongolia 40
Montserrat 14
Morken, Kimberly 33
Morocco 10, 14, 25, 27, 29, 35, 36,
    39, 52, 57
Morton, Louis 22
Mosvick, Melissa 52
Mozambique 45
Mulholland, David 9
Mulvihill, Richard 25
Murphy, Bertie Lee 56
Muskie, Edmund 30
Mutual Security Appropriation Act 2
Myers, Cynthia 11

N

Namibia 39, 40, 44, 46
National Academy of Sciences 23, 24
National Council of Returned Peace
    Corps Volunteers 28
National Peace Corps Association 28,
    37, 47, 51
National Returned Peace Corps Volun-
    teers Conference 11
Nelson, Peter 14
Nepal 9, 11, 13, 22, 32, 34, 41, 46, 52
Nettesheim, Chad 45
Neuberger, Richard L. 1
Nicaragua 15, 29, 40
Niger 9, 23, 33, 34, 43, 45
Nigeria 8, 9, 12, 13, 15, 21, 41, 43
Nitahara, Diane 13

Niue 42, 49
Nonnemacker, Joseph 19
Nordmann, William 41

O

Oâ€™Brien, John 15
Oâ€™Brien, Shaun 34
Oâ€™Donnell, Kevin 21, 22
Oâ€™Reilly, Patrick 18
Oâ€™Sullivan, Blythe Ann 54
Ohl, Daniel 39
Olson, William 13
Oman 23, 33
Orton, Jeffrey 43
Osborne, Dorothy 38
Ota, Dennis 22
Overholtzer, Paul 20
Owens, Robert 27

P

Pakistan 2, 8, 9, 13, 14, 37, 39, 40
Panama 10, 20, 21
Papua New Guinea 48
Paraguay 14, 38, 43
Parker, Robert 24
Parrott, John 12
Pasmore, Judith 47
Passman, Otto 21
Pastuszak, Robert 25
Payton, Carolyn R. 26, 28
Peace Corps
    20th anniversary 30, 31
    25th anniversary 34, 35
    30th anniversary 39, 40, 64
    40th anniversary 47
    50th anniversary 59
    Africa 1, 2, 8, 10, 22, 26, 35, 36, 44,
        46, 47, 58, 63, 64
    application 8, 19, 23, 26, 45, 56, 59
    book about ix, x, 4, 5, 8, 9, 16, 21,
        26, 27, 33, 37, 39, 44, 46, 47,
        49, 51, 54, 56, 58
    budget 13, 17, 20, 21, 22, 30, 31,
        57, 59

creation of 7
Crisis Corps 43, 44, 45, 53, 64
Fellows Program 34, 38, 43, 59, 64
film about 17, 35, 43, 52, 57, 69
five year limit 49, 50, 51, 52, 58
handbook 16, 47
HIV/AIDS 36, 41, 46, 48, 50, 55
independent 15, 21, 32
interns 30
library x, 4, 5, 14, 38, 56, 57, 63,
    69, 70
museum 4, 5, 54
New Directions 16, 20, 62
not independent 21
number of countries served 9, 10,
    12, 20, 22, 24, 25, 26, 29, 33,
    34
oppostition to director nomination
    48
recruiting x, 9, 14, 16, 19, 20, 23,
    24, 26, 27, 28, 30, 35, 43, 46,
    48, 53, 57, 62
report on 23, 62, 65, 66, 67, 69, 70
semi-independence 28
spplication 42
stamp 15, 21, 35, 46, 59
use of computers 33, 40, 41, 42, 53
Washington D.C. 16, 17, 19, 20, 21
Women in Development 25, 42, 44
World Wise Schools 37, 43, 46
Peace Corps Act 8, 26, 31, 49
Peace Corps Crossroads 44
Peace Corps News 8, 9
Peace Corps Online 47
Peace Corps staff
  anti-war 17
  co-country directors 26, 29
Peace Corps Times 27, 33, 38, 41, 48,
    55
Peace Corps Volunteer
  anti-war 13, 17, 18, 19, 49, 50, 68
  as business trainers 33
  attrition 3, 8, 11, 12, 15, 16, 19, 22,
    27, 29, 31, 34, 39, 44, 45, 53
  average age 8, 13, 16, 22, 27, 37,

    42, 54
culture shock 11
death 3, 9, 10, 11, 12, 14, 15, 18,
    19, 21, 22, 23, 24, 25, 27, 29,
    30, 31, 32, 33, 34, 35, 36, 37,
    38, 39, 40, 41, 42, 43, 44, 45,
    46, 47, 48, 49, 51, 52, 53, 54,
    55, 56, 57, 60
evacuation of 13, 33, 39, 40, 44, 55
film about 52, 57, 58
fisheries 29, 35, 36
HIV/AIDS 10, 16, 41, 47, 53, 54, 55
increased violence against 51
kidnap of 10, 26, 28
loan forgiveness 35
measuring success 4
medical and technical support x,
    12, 21, 24, 28, 29, 36, 44, 57,
    58, 59
military service 12, 14
minority 16, 27, 30, 42, 45, 54
over age 50 2, 13, 24, 27, 30, 37,
    42, 45, 53, 54
ratio men/women 3, 10, 16, 23, 24,
    26, 27, 37, 42, 45, 54
spies 8, 54, 55
staging 11, 19, 29, 30
tests 7, 8, 12, 14, 18, 19
training 3, 8, 10, 11, 12, 13, 14, 15,
    16, 17, 20, 21, 22, 23, 25, 26,
    28, 29, 30, 31, 33, 36, 42, 44,
    47, 58, 59, 61, 62, 65, 67
use of computers 45, 48, 52, 53, 56,
    58
use of radio 44
violence against 3, 4, 28, 40, 44, 49,
    51, 54, 58, 59
weapon against communist threat 8,
    10, 26, 31, 32
work by sector 3, 9, 10, 11, 16, 19,
    20, 23, 24, 26, 27, 28, 29, 42,
    44, 45
World Map Project 36, 58, 64
worldwide number of 3, 4, 9, 10, 11,
    12, 13, 15, 16, 19, 20, 22, 23,

24, 25, 26, 27, 28, 29, 30, 31,
32, 33, 34, 35, 36, 38, 39, 40,
41, 42, 43, 45, 46, 47, 48, 49,
50, 52, 53, 54, 55, 56, 59
Peace Corps Worldwide 56
Peace Corps Writers 46, 52, 55, 56
Pearson, Dennis 14
Pearson, Marcia 14
Percy Amendment 25
Periard, Michael 21
Perkins, Cecil 25
Peru 9, 13, 18, 19, 24, 25, 49
Pfaffenberger, Layne 42
Pfost, Dennis 24
Philippines 8, 9, 10, 12, 14, 18, 25,
29, 32, 34, 35, 36, 39, 41, 46,
52, 54
Phillips, Karen 46
Pickens, Hugh 70
Pillsbury, Wyatt 48
Pinney, Charles 25
Point Four Program 1
Point Four Youth Corps 1
Poirier, Walter J. 48, 51
Poland 39, 44, 48
Pollock, Craig 22
Presnal, Steven 32
Prior, Roy 25
Privacy Act 24
Provini, Rosenne 25
Puerto Rico 24
Puzey, Catherine 57

Q

Quigley, Kevin 70
Quiton, Juanita 37

R

Radley, Lawrence 9
Ragno, Marsha 21
Raimondo, Lucille 43
Raymaker, Mark 15
Reagan, Ronald 34, 63
Redmann, James 13

Reiser, William 14
Republic of Congo 40
Republic of the Congo 45
Returned Peace Corps Volunteer
anti-war 19, 50
Peace Corps Experience Special
Collection 5, 56
Reuss, Henry S. 1
Rice, Andrew E. 2
Ritger, Robert 22
Roberts, John Douglas 54
Roberts, Valeria 21
Robillard, Gerald 24
Robinson, Linda 23
Rodgers, Susan 20
Rodriguez, Annika 44
Rogers, Varina 41
Rolfs, Jeremy 45
Romania 40
Roosevelt, Theodore 1
Rose, Jennifer 47
Rosser, Denise 24
Ross, Troy 13
RPCV Writers 37
RPCV Writers & Readers 39
Rubin, David 30
Rubin, Jennifer 34
Ruppe, Loret Miller 31, 37
Russia 39, 40, 41, 51
Russomanno, Grace 25
Rwanda 25, 41, 56
Ryan, James 22

S

Saltwick, Catherine 56
Sanftleben, Lesa 34
Sao Tome e Principe 32
Scataloni, Patricia 52
Schaeffer, David 39
Schaffer, William 34
Scharninghausen, Kyrstin 44
Schneider, Mark L. 46, 48
Schutzius, Margaret 38
Schwartz, Frederick 19

Searles, P. David x, 70
Senate Foreign Relations Committee
   48
Senegal 10, 23, 32, 35, 36, 42
Seychelles 24, 44
Sheriff, Joseph 33
Sherman, Mathew 37
Shine, Henry George 13
Shippee, Andrew 43
Shriver, Robert Sargent Jr 7, 12, 30,
   48, 68
Shuler, Henry 18
Sierra Leone 9, 21, 25, 29, 30, 35, 41,
   42, 60
Simmons, Gareth 12
Simpson, Timothy 46
Slovak Republic 39, 49
Smith, Audrey 35
Smith, Sandra 18
Solomon Islands 21, 29, 35, 47
Somalia 32
Somali Republic 9, 19
South Africa 44, 45
South Korea 12, 31
Spratt, Paul 22
Sri Lanka 9, 11, 14, 19, 33, 45
Stafford, Jeannette 18
St. Christopher/Nevis 14
Stedman, Laura 44
Stilson, Dennis 27
St. Lucia 8, 9, 35
Stout, James 14
Streb, Mark 34
Strong, Terry 33
St. Vincent 14
Sudan 32, 33, 34, 36
Summers, Harold 25
Suriname 43, 54
Swaziland 17, 19, 32, 37, 44, 51
Swenson, Dale 9
Sykes, Richard 26
Sylvester, Michele 42

T

Tanzania 8, 9, 13, 15, 17, 19, 29, 39,
   48, 57
Teates, Joseph 36
Thailand 8, 9, 13, 32, 34, 36, 37
The Volunteer 9
Thompson, Christine 27
Thornton, Agatha 21
three main goals 4
Thyne, Jesse 47
Togo 9, 12, 13, 22, 27, 33, 34, 37, 42
Tonga 14, 15, 25, 35, 52, 53
Traub, Susan 14
Truman, Harry 1
Tschetter, Ronald A. 53, 56
Tunisia 9, 37, 39, 40, 44
Turkey 9, 14
Turkmenistan 41, 55
Turks/Caicos Islands 30
Turneer, Charles 34
Turner, Roderic 23
Tuvalu 24, 35, 45

U

Uganda 11, 22, 23, 40, 46, 47
Ukraine 41, 46, 54
United Nations 32, 39
United Nations Peace Corps 15, 20
University of California Berkeley 14
University of Michigan 2, 30, 59
Update 26, 62
Uruguay 10, 24, 40, 45
USAID 3, 31, 35, 36
Uzbekistan 41, 48, 52, 55

V

Vanuatu 39, 54
Vasquez, Gaddi H. 48, 51, 53, 67
Vaughn, Jack 12, 13, 16
Vazquez, Salvador 15
Venezuela 9, 27
Verloo, Etienne Victor 46
Virgin Islands 23
VISTA 10, 21, 35
Volunteer 17, 19, 21

Vonfoerster, Johnnes 12

W

Waldinger, Natalie 48
Wald, Karen 42
Warren, Robert 27
Weber, Donald 43
Weeks, James 22
Weiss, Rick 52
Weland, Robert 13
Western Samoa 14
West, William L. 22
White, Debora 27
Whitfield, Robert 22
Wilcox, Gary 27
Williams, Aaron S. 56
Willis, John 19
Wiseman, Gloey 40
Wolfe, Peter 34
Wolf, Louise 25

Wood, James 33
Wood, Michael 33
Woodward, Mitchell 30
Wright, John 35

Y

Yale University 48
Yemen 23, 39, 42

Z

Zaire 22, 23, 24, 34, 36
Zambia 41, 49, 52
Zbitnoff, Alexei 15
Zech, Robert 12
Zimbabwe 40, 48, 49
Zimmerman, Polly 25
Zink, Virginia 15

CPSIA information can be obtained
at www.ICGtesting.com
Printed in the USA
BVOW04s0433221116

468581BV00001B/43/P

9 781462 017003